The Feminine Irony

*Women on Women
in Early-Nineteenth-Century
English Literature*

THE FEMININE IRONY

Women on Women in Early-Nineteenth-Century English Literature

Lynne Agress

UNIVERSITY
PRESS OF
AMERICA

LANHAM • NEW YORK • LONDON

To my parents

Contents

Preface

If anyone thinks that the theme of this work — that women writers and intellectuals use their influence to perpetuate society's biases against women — is anachronistic, let him or her take a look around.

At a recent meeting of professional women, it was amazing to see highly successful older women — women who had slowly struggled up the ladder from subservient positions — who were now reluctant to help other women, particularly those who were younger than they and who were working in their own fields. Their tendency to view themselves apart from their sex, and thus to take on traditional masculine traits and opinions, was also interesting. These particular women chose to sit together and seemed to view with disdain any current changes in administrative policies and hiring procedures that would aid women and minorities. That they had made it was what counted.

During this meeting, at which slides were shown, the projector suddenly broke down. A very successful literary agent loudly agreed with a veteran feature writer that if a man were operating the machine, it would not have gone on the blink. And so the story goes.

Women are inclined to view women as subordinates. Women patients seek male physicians; women actresses, male directors; women secretaries, male bosses. Although the roles of some women have become more complex and diversified in our society, women's attitudes, in many cases, have not really changed.

This study of early-nineteenth-century British women may help to generate some new insights into the age-old feminine irony.

Acknowledgments

I wish to thank my former adviser, Professor Richard Haven, at the University of Massachusetts, Amherst, who originally suggested that I investigate early-nineteenth-century British women for the subject of my dissertation, which has been developed into this work.

I am also grateful to him and to Professors Joyce Berkman and Ellsworth Barnard at the University of Massachusetts for their valuable comments and suggestions while I was writing the dissertation.

To Gordon B. Lea I am most indebted for his criticisms and extensive commentary, particularly on the earlier versions of the work. Finally, I thank Charlotte Seitlin for her excellent editorial guidance, which enabled me to give the book its final form.

Introduction

*It is not the inferiority of women that has
caused their historical insignificance: it is
rather their historical insignificance that has
doomed them to inferiority.*[1]
— Simone de Beauvoir

Regardless of class, most English women passively, perhaps even eagerly, accepted a secondary, and therefore "insignificant," social, economic, and political role in the early nineteenth century. A few voiced their dissatisfaction with the status quo by protesting in print — but to little or no avail. Mary Wollstonecraft's *Vindication of the Rights of Women*, published in 1792, was one such protest, and an important one, but most of her women readers, instead of applauding her advocation of new freedoms for women, criticized and ridiculed her as heretical and socially dangerous.

One correspondent to the *Lady's Monthly Museum* complained that her four daughters

had always conducted themselves in the most exemplary fashion until they read *Rights of Women*. Thereupon the formerly proper young ladies had become lamentably and indecorously masculine. The eldest daughter now joined in the hunt with men, groomed her own horse, and wagered that she could outride any man in the neighbourhood. The second daughter, taking a bookish turn, seldom spoke without quoting from some classic and regularly held debates in her study. The third young lady developed such a passion for anatomy and vivisection that it was impossible to keep a dog or cat in the house. The youngest daughter, who became a devotee of military exercises, went about boasting that she was strong enough to knock down an ox.

This concerned mother may have been truthful enough, but Mary Wollstonecraft's *Vindication* alone can hardly be held responsible for so curious a series of metamorphoses in her offspring. At best, one might speculate that *Vindication* prompted these young women to act out their own human potential. The letter, however, indicates the intense — even exaggerated — emotionalism of the antifeminists. What is more, it points up their real fear that equality for women would make women masculine.

Naturally, *Vindication* and the few comparable pieces it inspired also triggered negative responses in men, as is illustrated by the comments of a *Gentleman's Magazine* reviewer. Referring to Anne-Frances Randall's *Letter to the Women of England, on the Injustice of Mental Subordination*, he writes, with no small degree of disdain, that "in the general confusion of ideas, religious, moral, and political we are not surprised to find claims set up for the female sex, unsupported we must not say by *prescription*, but we are justified in saying by *reason*." He adds: "Mrs. Randall avows herself of the school of Wollstencroft [*sic*]; and that is enough for all who have any regard to decency, order, or prudence, to avoid her company." The indictment seems disproportionate, but the reference to decency, order, and prudence is illuminating. Any interest in equality for women was considered morally wrong, destructive of social unity, imprudent, and lacking in caution and wisdom. Even today this idea remains the core of the antifeminist position. Female individuality had little room in a male-dominated society in which most women accepted the traditional male view. When it revealed itself, it was attacked and ridiculed as abnormal and unnatural.

Whether literature follows life or life imitates literature, woman's role in society and woman's role in literature tended to reinforce each other. Until the late eighteenth century, however, most books about women were written by men. A few novels about women by women had appeared, but they were not widely read. Besides Aphra Behn, who lived from 1640 to 1689, and, according to British scholar R. B. Johnson, is thought to be the first actual novelist (she wrote *Oroonoko: or, The History of the Royal Slave* in 1688), there were three women writers who preceded Fanny Burney, who became the first acclaimed woman novelist. One was Eliza Haywood (1688-1751), who wrote several novels "of intrigue and contemporary scandal," as well as *The History of Miss Betsy Thoughtless* (1751), a novel that traces the development of an inexperienced girl into a sophisticated young lady in London society, and which, in fact, gave Fanny Burney the idea for *Evelina.* Another eighteenth-century woman writer was Mary de la Riviere (1663-1724), whose work *The Power of Love in Seven Novels*—which features such titles as "The Fair Hypocrite" and "The Wife's Resentment"—is a series of "pretentious romances of intrigue" with "unreal sentiment," but, on the whole, is actually quite "conventional." A third woman author, Sarah Fielding, Henry Fielding's sister, who lived from 1714 to 1768, wrote a mediocre multivolume, moralistic novel inspired by Richardson's *Pamela*, called the *Adventures of David Simple in Search of a Faithful Friend.* "The friend" is a beautiful and amiable female.[2]

With the publication of Fanny Burney's *Evelina* in 1778, a radical change occurred: women began to write about themselves. There were actually hundreds of women writing and publishing during the period from 1780 to 1825, yet very little has been said about them or their work, or about the insights that they provided into the condition of women at the time.

With the exception of Jane Austen, who is not discussed here because of the attention that she has received elsewhere and because she was not particularly involved in female literary society, hardly any of the women writers of this period have received adequate attention. Yet writers such as Maria Edgeworth, Fanny Burney, Elizabeth Inchbald, Amelia Opie, Elizabeth Hamilton, Jane West, Ann Taylor, Anna L. Barbauld, Hannah More, Sydney Owenson Morgan, Charlotte Bury, Mary Russell Mitford, Sarah Trimmer, Mary Martha Butt Sherwood, Dorothy Wordsworth, Hester Stanhope, as well as Ann Radcliffe, Mary Wollstonecraft, and Mary Shelley, taken together, have made a significant contribution to literary history as well as to women's history.

Fictional and nonfictional books by women were read almost exclusively by a feminine audience. Although women writers were often discriminated against by male readers and critics, the women, with few exceptions, did little or nothing to challenge this discrimination. Ironically, they reinforced the passive, inferior, feminine stereotype in their writings as well as in their public statements.

But before we consider how woman's role was both reflected and defined by the female authors of the late eighteenth and early nineteenth centuries, it is important to understand how woman's role was defined by society, by class considerations, and by family structure.

The time of the Industrial Revolution was unique. Middle- and upper-class women, who functioned primarily in the drawing room, having no political rights and few economic ones, were regarded as the property of their husbands. Working-class women and their children labored long hours in factories and on farms, performing men's work but receiving "apprenticeship" wages. A few, upon the death of their husbands, even performed managerial jobs.

These hardworking women were far from being looked upon as pillars of feminine society, but female authors of books on education, etiquette, religion, and children's stories — all of which advocate, explicitly or implicitly, woman's submission — were. Denied a male audience, early-nineteenth-century women wrote for themselves, for children, and for other

women. Their greatest body of work was the novel, which, according to long-standing convention, was called "the female
genre." Indeed, to many female readers the novel provided all
the information on how a woman should conduct her life.
Whereas nearly all of the heroines are alike—pious, passive,
and beautiful, the subjects of the novels differ: there are
subgenres. Women wrote novels of manners, as well as
domestic fiction, regional and exemplary novels, and Gothic
novels. The critical responses to these novels were as
stereotyped as the female characters. Male critics, in the many
periodicals of the period, endorsed the portrayal of passive
heroines.

Consequently, the historical background, and the examina-
tion of women writers and of the literary treatment of women
in general, should not only add to an understanding of the
early-nineteenth-century woman but also illuminate further
her role during the Victorian period, when women were first
beginning to gain some rights, and when women writers, albeit
very few, appealed for the first time to male as well as to female
audiences. And finally, an awareness of the problems of
woman as her own worst enemy and of the dangers inherent in
stereotyping roles of women as well as of men may help us to
understand some of the problems that we face in our own
society.

NOTES

[1]Simone de Beauvoir, *The Second Sex*, ed. and trans. H. M. Parshley (New York:
Modern Library, 1968), p. 132.
[2]Reginald Brimley Johnson, *The Woman Novelists* (London: W. Collins Sons & Co.,
1918), pp. 2-3, and Ernest A. Baker, *A Guide to the Best Fiction in English* (New
York: Macmillan Co., 1913), pp. 10, 15.

The Feminine Irony

*Women on Women
in Early-Nineteenth-Century
English Literature*

1
Ladies of Labor
and Ladies of Leisure

*Do with me as you choose. I am utterly in your
power. I am a woman. You are a man.*[1]
— Lady Mary Wortley Montagu

England has never been without a class system. But while men
of the lower classes were often clearly discriminated against,
women suffered a double bias — one involving class, and the
other, perhaps the more debilitating, involving gender. Some
degree of social mobility has always been possible, but in
nineteenth-century England sexual mobility was practically
nonexistent.

Mary Wollstonecraft, in *A Vindication of the Rights of
Women*, sought to describe, at least in part, the state of ignorance and servility to which women were condemned by
their social roles and training. *Vindication*, generally scorned
and often unread by its critics, focused on the same theme that
Elizabeth Janeway would develop nearly two hundred years
later in her illuminating work *Man's World, Woman's
Place* — that what most women need is control over their own
lives. Mary Wollstonecraft's work reflected a widespread

21

revolutionary trend and, although this trend had little direct, immediate effect on women's status, its indirect, ultimate influence justifies a brief account of it.

Hannah More (1745-1833), a prolific writer of religious and moral works for women, wrote that she had been "much pestered to read the *Rights of Women*, but was invincibly resolved not to do it." She attacked the title for being "fantastic" and expresed her hatred for "metaphysical jargon." But she was actually against the book's advocacy of freedom, for she went on: "I am sure I have as much liberty as I can make good use of, now I am an old maid: and when I was a young one, I had, I dare say, more than was good for me."[2]

Many men, like some women, wanted more control over their own lives, for the uncompromising power that they exercised over their wives and children was not enough. But, unlike most women, they were determined to do something about it. Men wanted to be able to participate in lawmaking and to determine their own destinies, and the sooner the better. As a result, the stability that characterized most of eighteenth-century England was replaced by an unrest that precipitated change, one that began to affect England and other European countries during the late eighteenth and early nineteenth centuries, at the time of the so-called Romantic Period or Age of Revolution. The often strident demands for greater freedom voiced in the American colonies, in Ireland, and in France, threatened, both directly and indirectly, England's stability.

The American Revolution began in 1775 with the colonists expressing their desire, later recorded in the Declaration of Independence, for "life, liberty, and the pursuit of happiness." They elected George Washington the first president of the United States on April 30, 1789, and proceeded to govern themselves. The Patriots were determined to demonstrate the doctrines of Baron de Montesquieu and John Locke—that no one system of government suited all countries. "Laws should be in relation to the climate of each country," said Montesquieu, "to the religion of the inhabitants, to their inclinations, riches, numbers, commerce, manners and customs."[3] Locke agreed that man can best function in a state of equality "wherein all the power and jurisdiction is reciprocal, [with] no one having more than another."[4] But Locke's intellectually honest quest for greater freedom was fundamentally myopic. He did not include women and children in his definition of those who should enjoy equality.

Trouble with Ireland, which had been an intermittent problem in England since Stuart times, flared up again in the 1780s with the Irish protest against British political and religious oppression. Britain declared the Irish Parliament autonomous. The Irish Catholics were allowed to purchase land, but, ironically, they were denied the right to vote. In the uprising that resulted from this sanction, the Irish Parliament was abolished, and Ireland, in the Act of Union of 1800, was once again subjugated to Britain's rule.

In 1792 France declared war on the king of Bohemia and Hungary, in what was called a war "of peoples against kings."[5] A year later this conflict involved not only England, but practically all of Europe. It lasted, with some uncomfortable pauses, until June 1815, when Napoleon was finally defeated at Waterloo.

England was particularly susceptible to reverberations of these three conflicts — economically, ideologically, and politically. In fact, during the period of the 1780s through the 1820s, the political situation in England was deplorable. George III, for example, Shelley's "mad, blind, despised and dying" tyrant-cum-milksop, reigned — a reign that, for some sixty years, alternated between periods of feeble mismanagement and tyrannical control. When the monarch became insane, his son, George IV, the prince regent and liberalism's archenemy, took the scepter and ruled until 1830.

As a result of revolutionary terrorism and repression in France, a disillusionment with reform followed in both France and England, bringing to the fore a powerful group of conservatives. On the other hand, liberal factions, impressed with the revolutionary credo of liberty and equality, sought to apply laissez-faire policies to economics, to broaden civil rights, and to instigate social reform—reform that in many cases took nearly half a century to effect but that eventually did come about.[6] Reform was also influenced by an important religious revival, Evangelicalism, which began in England in the mid-eighteenth century. A type of "rejuvenated Protestantism," it spread from the University of Cambridge to the manufacturing districts of the industrial Midlands and the North. It sought to reform not only the Church but also national morality.[7] Evangelicalism challenged both the established church and the social elite. Although the most famous group of Evangelicals, the Clapham Sect, advocated a basic conservatism, accepting the "hierarchical assumption and prejudices of nearly all of the upper classes of their time," they were, nevertheless, critical of Regency politics. Their major effort was devoted to helping the poor. The founding of Sunday schools, in which reading was taught to the poor, and the abolition of the slave trade are the two humanitarian activities for which they are best known. The Evangelicals also tried to relieve oppression of children in factories, and, by an Act of Parliament, they attempted to improve the condition of children employed as chimney sweeps in London.

Reacting against the moral licentiousness of the eighteenth century, the Evangelicals advocated self-restraint through order and self-discipline, and this quality manifested itself generally in the emerging middle class and, specifically, in the middle-class family. During the late eighteenth and early nineteenth centuries, then, ferment of all kinds was in the air, and this ferment also involved women.

The French Revolution, with its ideal of liberty, equality, and fraternity, stimulated Mary Wollstonecraft to write her *Vindication*, for she concluded chapter 2 by stating that "as sound politics diffuse liberty, mankind, including women, will become more wise and virtuous."[8] In a piece on Mary Wollstonecraft in *The Common Reader*, Virginia Woolf says:

"The [French] Revolution was not merely an event that had happened outside her; it was an active agent in her own blood. She had been in revolt all her life — against tyranny, against law, against convention. The reformers' love fermented within her."[9]

The emerging Industrial Revolution, which defined and separated social classes more rigidly, caused many more women to enter the labor force, ultimately bringing about the first changes in woman's role in the nineteenth century. Although woman's participation in political and ideological revolutions was minimal, her role in agriculture and industry was much more significant and influential.

Beginning in the mid-eighteenth century, more and more women began to work on farms. The Enclosure Acts were greatly responsible for this change. Enclosures, which in medieval times were used to extend sheep pastures, now were used to increase crop land. In the eighteenth century Parliament had passed hundreds of individual enclosure acts affecting many small farmers who could not exist without their right to use common land, and who could not afford to purchase either the land or the equipment necessary to become landlords themselves. No longer able to live independently, to pasture a cow or pig, or to gather fuel, the cottagers and their wives and children were forced to labor. Approximately forty-five thousand women working in agriculture, for instance, were involved mainly in dairy farming, but they also weeded, planted, and reaped crops, led horses at the plough, and fed livestock. In addition to the hardships of manual work, women also had to contend with gang-masters, men who, once laborers themselves, profited from stealing and reselling provisions to gang members, and who often assaulted the women sexually.[10] (In *Against Our Will: Men, Women, and Rape* [1975] Susan Brownmiller traces the history of rape, which, then as today, was often requisite for employment.)

Women left their cottages not only to toil in fields, but also to labor in factories. Women worked in many industries, but principally in the textile industry.[11] While some women worked in cotton factories, others in the industry did piecework at home.[12] The latter worked long hours in dimly lit cottages, since many could hardly afford candles. In England, dependence on the sun for light was and is precarious, and eyestrain was one of many occupational ills from which women suffered. Their homes were damp, dingy, and overcrowded. There were few or no sanitary facilities, and such diseases as typhoid were rampant. What is more, while working-class women's strength was taxed by too little sleep—sixteen to eighteen hours was a normal day's work—and by excessive childbearing, it was further weakened by a scarcity of food and by poor nutrition. Few cottage laborers could afford a healthful diet, and most had little time to prepare balanced meals.

Unpleasant and primitive as the rural family's existence was, however, the factory system—where women assisted men in producing cloth, as well as buttons, buckles, bolts, pins, and innumerable other articles—was even worse. In Book 8 of *The Excursion*, Wordsworth poignantly treats the plight of the mother whose entire family must do factory work in order to subsist, perhaps even to survive:

> The Mother left alone, —no helping hand
> To rock the cradle of her peevish babe,
> No daughters round her, busy at the
>   wheel,
> Or in dispatch of each day's little growth
> Of household occupation; no nice arts
> Of needle-work; no bustle at the fire,
> Where once the dinner was prepared with
>   pride;
> Nothing to speed the day, or cheer the
>   mind;
> Nothing to praise, to teach, or to command!

(ll. 267-75)

Worst of all, men made twice the wages that women made
for the same work. Actually, for the precision work that the
textile industry required, women and children, with their
smaller hands, were much more adept, but since women and
children were always considered mere apprentices and assistants—"subsidiaries without technical training," as Ivy Pinchbeck puts it—they were miserably underpaid no matter how
impressive their output.[13]

Although most working-class women toiled at such back-
breaking jobs as "assistants to masons and bricklayers, . . .
labourers in brickyards and foundries, . . .load carriers to and
from markets, . . .rag sorters and cutters in paper mills, . . .
[and] cinder sifters and collecters of refuse," no job was more
brutal and brutalizing—nor, on the working-class scale of
work, less prestigious—than mining.[14] Even here, women
worked—and they worked underground in ironstone, copper,
and lead mines. Miners and their families were regarded by
everyone as "savages and outcasts," for their brutalized existence clearly reflected the bestiality of the labors in which
they were engaged. In *Coal Trade of Scotland*, for example,
the sufferings of women mineworkers are described. Indeed,
women were so exhausted from the strenuousness of their labor
that they wept. Up from the mine one came who was "groaning
under an excessive weight of coals, trembling in every nerve,
and almost unable to keep her knees from sinking under her."
As she came up, "she said in a most plaintive and melancholy
voice: 'O Sir, this is sore, sore work. I wish to God that the first
woman who tried to bear coals had broke her back and none
would have tried it again.' "[15] The women in the mines worked
incredibly long hours, occasionally as many as twenty-four at a
stretch. Pregnancy was no deterrent, and not infrequently a
woman would ascend from the pit, where she had been working all day, with a newly delivered infant as black with soot as
its mother.[16]

Despite these brutal working conditions, reform was extremely difficult; most women workers were both too in-

timidated and too oppressed to protest. However, the Factory Act of 1819 precluded children of nine years of age or younger from working in factories and limited the working day for women to twelve hours. This reform, explains E. P. Thompson in *The Making of the English Working Class*, was in part precipitated by a small group of rebels in the textile districts who "gave rise to the earliest widespread participation by working women in political and social agitation." Furthermore, Thompson claims that "the war years, with their increased demand for labour not only in the spinning mills but also at the hand loom, accelerated the process of social agitation."[17]

Predictably, women reformers faced strong opposition. The London *Courier* described "the 'petticoat reformers' of Manchester as 'degraded females,' guilty of 'the worst prostitution of the sex, the prostitution of the heart,' 'deserting their station,' and putting off the 'sacred characters' of wife and mother 'for turbulent vices of sedition and impiety.' "[18] On the other hand, William Cobbett, a somewhat conservative member of Parliament, though he opposed the vote for women, had no second thoughts about coming to the female reformers' aid: "Just as if women were made for nothing but to cook oat-meal and to sweep a room! Just as if women had no minds! Just as if Hannah More and the Tract Gentry had reduced the women of England to a level with the Negresses of Africa! Just as if England had never had a queen!"[19] Here Cobbett reflected the paradoxical attitude toward women of all classes.

Perhaps the advantages and disadvantages that resulted from the Industrial Revolution were, however, more significant. Thompson explains the contradiction: "On the one hand, the claim that the Industrial Revolution raised the status of women would seem to have little meaning when set beside the record of excessive hours of labour, cramped housing, excessive child-bearing and terrifying rates of child mortality." He continues: "On the other hand, the abundant opportunities for female employment in the textile districts gave to women the status of independent wage earners. The spinster or the widow was freed from dependence upon relatives or upon parish relief. Even the unmarried mother might be able, through the laxness of 'moral discipline' in many mills, to achieve an independence unknown before."[20]

Pinchbeck also demonstrates this paradoxical attitude. First she mentions that, under the Poor Laws, women were better off either married or with children since parishes gave them extra allowances; elsewhere, however, she states that "the most striking effect of the Industrial Revolution was. . .[woman's] distinct gain in social and economic independence."[21]

Closer scrutiny of these laws reveals that women's gains were not really so pronounced, for the underpaid, insecure female workers were the first to be let go during strikes and cutbacks. In addition, Pinchbeck explains that the "concentration of industry, which brought more employment and higher wages for women in districts where machinery was introduced, meant that many thousands of spinners in scattered, outlying rural parishes must ultimately lose all chance of employment."[22] Since these women were, in childhood, forced to work to help support their families, very few learned how to read or write. Working sixteen to eighteen hours a day, they were also ignorant of domestic duties and, as a result, were unable to obtain alternate jobs as maids or cooks. Consequently, crime and prostitution, starvation and suicide inevitably followed periods of unemployment. Readers of parish records were shocked at the large number of female vagrants. Indeed, among those impoverished women workers who grew up with little or no moral instruction or occupational training, "chastity was said to be at a sad discount, while prostitution was at a high premium."[23] An unescorted woman walking on the street was automatically taken to be a prostitute, and the "manners" shown toward her were often "free and menacing or worse."[24]

Actually, as nineteenth-century historian Robert Webb explains, "vice and prostitution which had flourished openly in the eighteenth century were driven underground by the spread of Evangelical morality in the nineteenth century," but, he adds, "not so far underground as to be invisible and unimportant."[25] Similarly, Walter Houghton, in *The Victorian Frame of Mind*, compares the bibliographies on prostitution published in England and Scotland between 1810 and 1840 with those published between 1840 and 1870 and finds that fewer appeared during the earlier period. Nevertheless, prostitution was considered "a transitory state, through which an untold number of British women [were]. . .ever on their passage."[26]

Helene Roberts, in her article "Marriage, Redundancy or Sin," comments on the masculine double standard that resulted in the wretched treatment of working-class women. Men of the middle and upper classes sexually exploited working-class women while their middle- and upper-class wives often rejected sex because of their piety.[27] The class bias of the sex market was also recognized by William Acton, a nineteenth-century physician who specialized in diseases of the urinary and generative organs—a man who became known through his writings on prostitution. Commenting on man's exploitation of women, Acton says:

> It cannot be denied by anyone acquainted with rural life that seduction of girls is a sport and habit with vast numbers of men, married. . .and single, placed above the ranks of labour. . . . Many such rustics of the middle class and men of parallel grades in country towns employ a portion of their spare time in the coarse, deliberate villainy of making prostitutes. . . . Men who themselves employ female labour, or direct it for others, have always ample opportunities of choice, compulsion, secrecy and subsequent intimidation, should exposure be probable and disagreeable. . .with these and with the gentlemen whose *dé'assement* is the contamination of town servants and *ouvriè'es*, the first grand engine is, of course, vanity.[28]

But all this is hardly a justifiable excuse.

In addition, Steven Marcus, in *The Other Victorians*, a treatment of the escapades of the anonymous author of *My*

Secret Life, points out that "most of the women whom he [the author] knows sexually, come from a single and fairly homogeneous population, since it is safe to say that both servants and prostitutes were by and large recruited from the same parts of society, the agricultural and urban laboring or working classes."[29] The main fact that Marcus discusses is that "the woman servant was the primary sexual opportunity of society before the twentieth century, and the innumerable variations upon the sexual encounters of masters and servants reflect this fact."[30]

Over five-hundred thousand lower-class women labored as domestic servants. They were expected to work seven days a week with time off only to attend church, and their "wages" were in the form of bed and board. In addition, they were often accosted sexually by both their male employers and their fellow workers. It is thus small wonder that many turned to prostitution for clothes and money.

Apparently a lone voice from the middle class, that of Mary Wollstonecraft in *Vindication,* expresses compassion for prostitutes. "Highly as I respect marriage as the foundation of almost every social virtue," she writes, "I cannot avoid feeling the most lively compassion for those unfortunate females who are broken off from society, and by one error torn from all those affections and relationships that improve the heart and mind. . . . Asylums and magdalens," she adds, "are not the proper remedies for those abuses. It is justice, not charity, that is wanting in the world!"[31]

What the class system makes quite clear, then, is that although not all women were brutally exploited sexually or industrially, there is no doubt that the majority of women, regardless of class, were in some way exploited. So far as women were concerned, "justice" was indeed "wanting." As the narrator of *My Secret Life* so aptly expresses it: "Women are all bought in the market from the whore to the Princess. The price alone is different and the highest price in money or rank obtains the woman."[32]

Whereas the lower-working-class woman spent virtually all of her time toiling in fields, dairies, factories, or mines, the middle-class woman spent nearly all of her time in the home, living, it is true, in idleness and luxury, but also as a hostage. John Langdon-Davies in *A Short History of Women* discusses all classes of women in his summary of their dilemma: "To puritanism and license, we have to add then parasitism as a growing cause of women's degredation and by adding a fourth cause, overwork, we round off the double antithesis. Underwork and overwork henceforth go hand in hand as shapers of women's history."[33]

Just as the Industrial Revolution was directly responsible for the plight of the oppressed working-class woman, so was it perhaps also a cause of the idleness of the middle-class woman. G. Kitson Clark in *The Making of Victorian England* defines the English middle class as "all the people who at any given moment came in income, or in social estimation, between the nobility and landed gentry on the one hand and the manual labourers on a weekly or daily wage on the other."[34]

With the advent in the early nineteenth century of the Industrial Revolution, the members of the middle class began to acquire wealth, comfort, and leisure time, and they became a formidable force in the community, determined, as they were, to represent the intelligence, morality, and refinement of the nation. Since the middle class did not possess rank or title, they had to rely exclusively on their appearance and behavior in order to project their affluence and to exert power. The transition from the perfect wife to the perfect lady was therefore very important to the middle-class family. One of the major distinctions between the lower middle class and the upper middle class involved the number of servants a woman employed. Leisure time, too, was considered to be a yardstick of status for a married woman. However, as J. A. and Olive Banks point out, "Emancipation from the constraints of the domestic routine should not be confused with emancipation from dependence upon the male members of the family."[35]

When a man became successful in a business or profession and could afford material possessions, he often treated his wife as one of his possessions. His sole desire was to dress her up, to keep her as an ornament. Mary Wollstonecraft refers sarcastically to this role. Middle-class woman "was created to be the toy of man, his rattle, and it must jingle in his ears whenever, dismissing reason, he chooses to be amused," she writes in *Vindication*.[36] Harriet Martineau, too, was aware of women's subordinate position, for she writes in 1823 that "women must be educated to be companions to men, instead of playthings or servants."[37]

But the "leisured lady" was "the hallmark of conspicuous consumption," and "the successful businessman delighted to demonstrate his success to the world by showing off his wife and daughters expensively clad, living a life of ease and elegance."[38]

The position of the nuclear family was an important factor in defining the role of the nineteenth-century middle-class woman. The family was supposed to be "a little sphere of peace and order to which [a man] could retreat,"[39] and it was considered a woman's duty to make the home a perfect place for her husband and children — the only place where they could escape from the cruel and competitive English society. But, as a modern critic suggests, the perfectionist expectations were arduous, and therefore it was small wonder that middle-class men philandered and that women found escape, or at least refuge, in reading novels.

The novel provided women with an escape from idleness and boredom — even though, ironically, many novelists stressed women's idle, domestic, and passive role. But this role was precisely what nineteenth-century men preferred and found desirable. Once a man reached marriageable age he kept remarrying whenever he found himself without a wife. Consequently, fertility in England from the mid-eighteenth century through the nineteenth was higher than in previous times. Author William Thompson brutally substantiates this statistic:

"The house is *his* [the husband's] with everything in it; and of
all fixtures the most abjectly his is his breeding machine, the
wife."[40]

In *An Inquiry into the Duties of the Female Sex*, first
published in 1796 and reissued in seven editions between then
and 1806, Thomas Gisborne defines, perhaps less grossly, the
triple role of the middle- and upper-class woman:

> First, [she must] contribute daily and hourly to the comfort
> of husband, of parents, of brothers and sisters, and of other
> relations, connections, and friends, in the intercourse of
> domestic life, under every vicissitude of sickness and health,
> of joy and affliction.
> Secondly, [she must] form and improve the general man-
> ners, dispositions, and conduct of the other sex, by society
> and example.
> Thirdly, [she must] model the human mind during the
> stages of its growth and fix. . . ,while it is still ductile, its
> growing principles of action; children of each sex being, in
> general, under maternal tuition during their childhood, and
> girls until they become women.[41]

Another striking example of essentially the same idea is
presented by Ray Strachey in *"The Cause": A Short History of
the Women's Movement in Great Britain*. "It was generally
agreed," she says of early-nineteenth-century English society,
"to be one of the self-evident laws of nature that men were
superior to women — mentally, physically and morally. Education, therefore, would be wasted upon them; responsibility
would overwhelm them, and work would make them ill. They
must be sheltered, protected, and indulged — so the theory ran.
They were the wives, or the mothers, or the daughters of some
man; that was their description and the real justification of
their existence."[42]

Clearly the ideal nineteenth-century middle-class woman
was a Galatea, made to order. She had to have four essential
traits, or, as Barbara Welter lists them in "The Cult of True
Womanhood," "cardinal virtues" — "piety, purity, sub-

missiveness and domesticity."[43] It was as simple as that. Middle-class women were supposed to behave like pasteboard characters in a morality play. The ideal female stereotype in early-nineteenth-century English society was religious. While men were involved in government, business, law, and other significant social endeavors, wives were required to pray for their husband's moral well-being and strength. The women's magazines also propagandized the religious female. An article in an issue of *Ladies Companion*, for example, argues that "woman never looks lovelier than in her reverence for religion and that, conversely, female irreligion is the most revolting feature in human character."[44] The piece is aptly titled "Female Irreligion." Middle-class girls were often entrusted to convents, where they were taught to perform "pious exercises" and were given exclusively religious instruction. Not surprisingly, Hannah More also thought that religion and chastity were most important in women, and she wrote several rather tedious books on the subject. Apparently, only Mary Wollstonecraft believed that "woman must serve and know herself as well as God and Man, and the ways of God must be justified to her as to her husband."

The second "cardinal virtue" was "purity," and the stress that this received prompts one to wonder why women ever married at all. Herein lies another contradiction: while middle-class women were supposed to be paragons of virtue (a "fallen woman" was a "fallen angel," unworthy of the celestial company of her sex),[45] marriage was regarded as the only desirable vocation for women. Women were taught that chasti-:y and modesty were to be used as "tools for the capture of men," as "bait which appealed to [men's] sensuality."[46] "Husbands were self-indulgent sexually and their wives submitted dutifully."[47] Mary Wollstonecraft, commenting on the hypocrisy of this preoccupation with chastity, writes: "If the honour of a woman, as it is absurdly called, be safe, she may neglect every social duty; nay, ruin her family by gaming and extravagance; yet still present a shameless front — for truly she is an honourable woman."[48] Women thus married for security, for comfort, and for social acceptance, and they bore children to maintain their position in their middle-class homes. In contrast, their husbands often shattered class lines, sometimes brutally, and certainly irresponsibly, in pursuit of selfish pleasure. This double standard is precisely what Mary Wollstonecraft means when she exclaims that "all the causes of female weakness as well as depravity. . .branch out of one grand cause — want of chastity in men!"[49]

But women's submissiveness only reinforced man's desire to dominate, and submissiveness was lauded as the most feminine of all virtues. A woman had to submit to God, to her husband, eventually even to her sons, and the more passive the acceptance the more it was glorified. "There is no animal," claimed Hannah More — ironically, a member of the Unitarian circle of advanced minds — "so much indebted to subordination for its good behavior as woman."[50] Women were actually warned, as Eve is warned by Adam in *Paradise Lost*, that if they rejected submissiveness, they would be guilty of seeking to destroy universal order. C. Willett Cunnington, commenting on the nineteenth-century woman, says that "a really sensible woman feels her dependence; she. . .is conscious of her inferiority and therefore grateful for support."[51] Lord Henry Home Kames, in his 1781 volume *Loose Hints Upon Education*, argues that women, "destined by nature to be obedient, ought to be disciplined early to bear wrongs without murmuring."[52]

Since pious, pure, submissive creatures could hardly lead in society, "domesticity" was, aptly, woman's final virtue. All the ladies' magazines and most novels argued for woman's passive position in the home: "The sphere of Domestic Life is the sphere in which female excellence is best displayed," says the anonymous author of *Woman as She Is and as She Should Be*. Any expression of interest by a woman in nondomestic matters, in gaining any personal rights, for instance, was suspect and labeled unfeminine. Yet actual housework and child care were discouraged and usually left to servants. The higher the class to which a woman belonged, the more servants she had. Truly prosperous women were for the most part idle, encouraged to do little more than arrange flowers, write letters, and supervise menus. Among women with more imaginative minds, correspondence alone provided a creative outlet. Such letters occasionally became memoirs or epistolary novels. Fanny Burney's *Evelina*, published in 1778, was but one of scores of the latter. Solid reading was discouraged, but religious biographies, women's magazines, and moralistic novels by acceptable authors — that is, by those who never mentioned sex or vice or who never discussed such subjects as politics or economics — were considered appropriate for women. Critic Maurice Quinlan writes that the main characters in Hannah More's novel, *Coelebs in Search of a Wife* (1809), "avoided all amusements, as if their virtue were made of such frail stuff that it could stand no trial."[53] If women were given the opportunity to read, what they read deprived them of any opportunity to think. As C. Willett Cunnington writes, "To be perfectly pure, the female mind. . .[in the nineteenth century] had to be perfectly blank."[54]

Yet middle-class women in the early nineteenth century were beginning to seek education. Finishing schools for women were being established everywhere. Typically, however, they resulted in contradictions. As did the Industrial Revolution, these schools served further to divide social classes — not only the working from the middle, but also the lower middle from the upper middle.

As early as 1694, Mary Astell proposed establishing a college for women, but over a century elapsed before any action was taken to make higher learning available to the female sex. Both middle- and upper-class women of the eighteenth century were concerned primarily with clothes, manners, dancing, card-playing, and entertaining. As Lady Mary Wortley Montagu said at the beginning of the eighteenth century: "We are taught to place all our art in adorning our outward forms."[55]

Since marriage was regarded as the only acceptable goal for a woman, schools were set up where girls were "trained. . .to get husbands."[56] Maria Edgeworth—who, as we shall see, failed to follow her own dictates—speaking of the proper education for a woman, writes: "Her mind must be enlarged, yet the delicacy of her manners must be preserved; her knowledge must be various, and her powers of reasoning unawed by authority; yet she must habitually feel that nice sense of propriety, which is at once the guard and charm of feminine virtue."[57] Edgeworth seems to be suggesting, although in a curiously contradictory fashion, that a woman should be free to accumulate knowledge as long as she does not neglect her domestic duties or compete with her husband.

Queens College for Women, the first women's college in England, was founded in 1848, but from about 1750 on women's boarding schools flourished, patronized mostly by the daughters of the socially ambitious middle class, the nouveau riche. The girls learned penmanship, some mathematics, and a smattering of French expressions. They also read "the more elegant English authors," such uncontroversial and bland writers as Hannah More, Sarah Pennington, and Anna L. Barbauld, all of whom never failed to describe the model female—chaste, submissive, virtuous.

Consequently, the schools' main emphasis fell on etiquette, dancing, deportment, and posture. An elitist writer in *Sentimental Magazine* even objected to teaching these to girls of the lower middle class, arguing that "it would be of much more consequence [that] they should be well instructed in how to wash the floor than to dance upon it."[58]

The girls were taught by spinsters of the upper middle class. These women, of whom Hannah More is the best known, were themselves products of the dualities embodied in contemporary womanhood. They sought to prepare young girls for the one acceptable women's vocation, marriage, but they themselves were single.[59] (When they reached middle age, however, they adopted the respectable title of *Mrs.*) Although they sought to condition women to idleness, they were actually rebelling against it by teaching. The greatest irony, however, lies in the fact that the underlying point of Hannah More's occupation was to teach women to be contented with their lot. As Hannah More herself put it, "I allow of no writing for the poor." Still, More, like hundreds of women instructors, by teaching women, were unconscious revolutionists, for as women became more knowledgeable, it was inevitable that they would also become dissatisfied with their boring, unproductive lives.

A few schools did attempt to prepare some women of the lower middle class to earn a living, but only in such conventional female occupations as teaching, governing children, or shopkeeping. A writer in *Meliora: A Quarterly Review of Social Sciences* suggests the vicious cycle that women's education constituted: "The present unsatisfactory position of women is partly the cause, partly the effect, of their imperfect education." He explains that "they are unfit for the duties of citizenship, because they are not trained for them; they are not trained because they are deemed unfit for them."[60]

The main advantage of such schools was their snob appeal. Even though the curriculum of boys' schools was distinctly superior, girls' schools were more costly. As a result, fewer girls could afford to attend, and the schools became very exclusive.

The position of middle-class women was certainly less unattractive than that of their working-class sisters, but legally they had no additional rights. Once married, middle-class women were virtually unable to obtain divorces even though they were starved, beaten, or otherwise abused. "If a woman be of so haughty a stomach that she will choose to starve rather than submit and be reconciled to her husband, she may take her own choice," stated Judge Hidy in *Manby v. Scot* in the Reign of Charles II, "and if a married woman who can have no goods of her own to live on will depart from her husband against his will, let her live on charity, or starve in the name of God."[61] Until 1857 divorce was obtainable only by means of a prohibitively expensive special Act of Parliament. Because wives could have neither money nor property legally, this procedure reinforced the double standard. The Act allowed a man to divorce his wife for adultery, but unless a woman could furnish convincing evidence of extreme cruelty or desertion, she was unable to obtain a divorce.

The following excerpt from an article that first appeared in the *Lancaster Herald* describes the even further humiliating "lower-class method of divorce":

Sale of a wife at Carlisle. — The inhabitants of this city lately witnessed the sale of a wife by her husband, Joseph Thompson, who resides in a small village about three miles distant, and rents a farm of about forty-two or forty-four acres. She was a spruce, lively, buxom damsel, apparently not exceeding twenty-two years of age, and appeared to feel a pleasure at the exchange she was about to make. They had no children during their union, and that, with some family disputes, caused them by mutual agreement to come to the resolution of finally parting. Accordingly, the bellman was sent round to give public notice of the sale, which was to take place at twelve o'clock; and this announcement attracted the notice of thousands. She appeared above the crowd, standing on a large oak chair, surrounded by many of her friends, with a rope or halter, made of straw, round her neck, being dressed in rather a fashionable country style, and appearing to some advantage. The husband, who was also standing in an elevated position near her, proceeded to put her up for sale, and spoke nearly as follows: — "Gentlemen, I have to offer to your notice my wife, Mary Anne Thompson, otherwise Williamson, whom I mean to sell to the highest and fairest bidder. It is her wish as well as mine to part for ever. I took her for my comfort, and the good of my house, but she has become my tormentor and a domestic curse, &c. &c. &c. Now I have shown you her faults and failings, I will explain her qualifications and goodness. She can read fashionable novels and milk cows; she can laugh and weep with the same ease that you can take a glass of ale; she can make butter, and scold the maid; she can sing Moore's melodies, and plait her frills and caps; she cannot make rum, gin, or whisky, but she is a good judge of their quality from long experience in tasting them, I therefore offer her, with all her perfections and imperfections, for the sum of fifty shillings." — After an hour or two, she was purchased by Henry Mears, a pensioner, for the sum of twenty shillings and a Newfoundland dog. The happy pair immediately left town together amidst the shouts and huzzas of the multitude, in which they were joined by Thompson, who, with the greatest good-humour imaginable, proceeded to put the halter, which his wife had taken off, round the neck of his Newfoundland dog, and then proceeded to the first public house where he spent the remainder of the day.[62]

To the middle-class female, however, there was little point to committing adultery, since usually she could not afford to live on her own. Until the Married Women's Property Act of 1870, a woman's land, goods, and money were automatically the property of her husband. Thus if husband and wife were to separate, everything belonged to the husband.[63]

In the early nineteenth century, women's rights and privileges were few indeed. The position of the upper-class woman was not much different from — and, in its own way, no less contradictory to — that of the middle-class woman. She had more servants, which reduced her household responsibilities, and, since governesses were a familiar adjunct of such homes, she had little contact with her children. Thus the upper-class woman had a limited choice — between insouciant boredom and a trivial social life. She could, after all, attend "acceptable" plays, and she could give parties and teas. Or she could engage in clandestine affairs with a variety of suitors, for among the aristocracy a good deal of sexual freedom was tacitly condoned. Many upper-class women kept lover-companions, what the Italians called *cavalier serventes,* who accompanied them to social functions when their husbands were away on business or were simply uninterested. But the emptiness of these women's lives was dangerous. Many fell hopelessly in love with their extramarital suitors and companions and were often brokenhearted when the relationships ended. It is to this plight of the unoccupied, upper-class woman that Byron refers when he writes in *Don Juan:*

Man's love is of man's life a thing apart,
  'Tis a Woman's whole existence; Man may range
The Court, Camp, Church, the Vessel, and the Mart;
  Sword, Gown, Gain, Glory offer, in exchange
Pride, Fame, Ambition, to fill up his heart,
  And few there are whom these can not estrange;
Men have all these resources, We but one —
To love again, and be again undone.
                                    (Canto 1, line 194)

Lady Caroline Lamb, who was involved in a liaison with
Lord Byron, wrote the following to a friend shortly after Byron
had ended their affair:

The only question I want you to solve is, shall I go abroad?
Shall I throw myself upon those who no longer want me, or
shall I live a good sort of a half kind of life in some cheap
street in a little way off, viz. the City Road, Shoreditch,
Camberwell, or upon the top of a shop, — or shall I give lectures to little children, and keep a seminary, and thus earn
my bread? or shall I write a kind of quiet, everyday sort of
novel, full of wholesome truths, or shall I attempt to be
poetical, and failing, beg my friends for a guinea apiece,
and their name, to sell my work, upon the best foolscap
paper; or shall I fret, fret, and die; or shall I be dignified
and fancy myself, as Richard the Second did when he picked
the nettle up — upon a thorn?[64]

Although the letter reveals a dramatic flamboyance, it also
catches the boredom and absence of choice of many
nineteenth-century women. Nevertheless, upper-class women
were often a target for the jealousy of middle- and lower-class
women, who, like Fanny Burney's Evelina, envied them their
"birth and fortune," which led to the "attainment of respect
and civility."
    At least one upper-class spinster managed to lead an in-
teresting and unconventional life: Lady Hester Stanhope, the

niece of William Pitt, with whom she lived. When he died and left her a substantial sum of money, she traveled through Europe and the Middle East. In Malta she took a lover eleven years her junior, who for three years was her traveling companion. Rumor has it that it was she who ended the affair. Afterward she spent her life receiving visitors and writing letters and memoirs. When her death was announced, "there was," according to Harriet Martineau, "a sense of relief — a sense of comfort that that restless and mysterious mind was asleep, and past the power of annoyance from without and misgiving from within."

In light of the social backdrop against which women of the early nineteenth century acted out their roles, it is hard to believe that any literature was ever produced by women. But it was, and by some exceptional women — women who managed to combine the intellectual power and perception of a Mary Wollstonecraft, the audacity of a Hester Stanhope, and the stamina of the working class in general.

NOTES

1. Iris Barry, *Portrait of Lady Mary Wortley Montagu* (New York: Bobbs-Merrill, 1928), p. 73.
2. Hannah More, *Memoirs of the Life and Correspondence of Mrs. Hannah More*, ed. William Roberts, 2 vols. (New York: Harper & Bros., 1837), 1:427.
3. Baron Charles Louis de Montesquieu, *The Spirit of the Laws*, trans. Thomas Nugent (New York: Appleton, 1949), bk. 1, chap. 3.
4. Eugen Weber, *A Modern History of Europe* (New York: W. W. Norton, 1971), p. 489, and Peter Laslett, *The World We Have Lost: England Before the Industrial Age*, 2d ed. (New York: Scribners, 1973), p. 190.
5. Weber, *History of Europe*, p. 525.
6. Humanitarian laws were not established until mid-nineteenth century. For example, the first general public health act was not passed until 1848. The British working-class male did not gain the right to vote until 1867, a generation after the wealthier middle class. Women, that is, all women, including those whose husbands did not own land and those who had no husbands, were not given the right to vote until 1928.
7. Elie Halévy, *A History of the English People in 1815* (London: Penguin, 1924), p. 249.

8. Mary Wollstonecraft, *A Vindication of the Rights of Women* (1792; reprint ed., New York: E. P. Dutton & Co., 1929), p. 42.

9. Virginia Woolf, *The Common Reader*, 2d ser. (London: Hogarth Press, 1932), p. 158.

10. Henry Hamilton, *England: A History of the Homeland* (New York: W. W. Norton, 1948), p. 324, and Ivy Pinchbeck, *Women Workers and the Industrial Revolution*, 1750-1850 (London: Routledge, 1930), p. 10.

11. According to an 1851 census, cotton workers totaled 255,000 men and 272,000 women. There were 171,000 male wool workers and 113,000 female workers. Linen and flax workers boasted 47,000 men and 56,000 women; and silk workers, 53,000 men and 80,000 women. G. Kitson Clark, *The Making of Victorian England* (New York: Atheneum, 1972), p. 113.

12. A census return of 1841 indicates that the largest group of women, a total of 712,493, were involved in domestic service. Some 115,425 worked in cotton manufacturing, and 89,079 in dressmaking and millinery. Cited in Hamilton, *England*, p. 324.

13. Pinchbeck, *Women Workers*, p. 2.

14. Ibid., p. 2, and Hamilton, *England*, p. 320.

15. From Bald, *Coal Trade of Scotland*, pp. 130-32, cited in Pinchbeck, *Women Workers*, pp. 252-53.

16. Finally in 1842 Lord Shaftesbury began agitating for legislation that would prevent labor by women in mines. After a long and bitter debate, the bill became law on August 10, 1842, and women were expelled from the mines — at least legally. Unfortunately, since these women had no other jobs, many insisted on remaining.

17. Edward P. Thompson, *The Making of the English Working Class* (New York: Vintage, 1963), p. 415.

18. Ibid., p. 417.

19. *Courier* 15 (July 1819), cited in Thompson, *Making of English Working Class*, p. 417.

20. Thompson, *Making of English Working Class*, p. 414.

21. Pinchbeck, *Women Workers*, p. 313.

22. Ibid., p. 156.

23. *Children's Employment Commission* (1843) xiv, pp. A10, A12, cited in Pinchbeck, *Women Workers*, pp. 310-12.

24. Clark, *Making of Victorian England*, p. 60.

25. Robert Webb, *Modern England: From the Eighteenth Century to the Present* (New York: Dodd, Mead & Co., 1971), p. 406.

26. Dr. William Acton, quoted by Steven Marcus, *The Other Victorians: A Study of Sexuality and Pornography in Mid-Nineteenth-Century England* (New York: Basic Books, 1966), p. 6.

27. Helene E. Roberts, "Marriage, Redundancy or Sin," *Suffer and Be Still: Women in the Victorian Age*, ed. Martha Vicinus (Bloomington: University of Indiana Press, 1972), p. 87.

28. William Acton, *Prostitution Considered in Its Moral, Social, and Sanitary Aspects* (1857; reprint ed., London: Frank Cass, 1972), p. 274.

29. Marcus, *The Other Victorians*, p. 129.

30. Mary Ellmann, *Thinking About Women* (New York: Harcourt, Brace & World, 1968), p. 127.

31. Wollstonecraft, *Vindication*, p. 79.
32. Marcus, *The Other Victorians*, p. 158.
33. John Langdon-Davies, *A Short History of Women* (New York: Viking Press, 1927), p. 324.
34. Clark, *Making of Victorian England*, p. 5.
35. J. A. and Olive Banks, *Feminism and Family Planning in Victorian England: Studies in the Life of Women* (New York: Schocken Books, 1964), p. 12.
36. Wollstonecraft, *Vindication*, p. 38.
37. Quoted in Alice S. Rossi, Introduction to *Mill's Essays on Sex Equality*, by John Stuart Mill and Harriet Taylor (Chicago: University of Chicago Press, 1970), p. 20.
38. Hamilton, *England*, p. 321.
39. Kirk Jeffrey, "The Family as Utopian Retreat from the City: The Nineteenth-Century Contribution," *The Family, Communes, and Utopian Societies*, ed. Sallie Teselle (New York: Harper & Row, 1971), p. 28.
40. From William Thompson, *An Appeal of One Half of the Human Race, Women, against the Pretensions of the Other Half, Men, to Retain Them in Political, and Thence in Civil and Domestic Slavery; in Reply to a Paragraph of Mr. Mill's Celebrated "Article on Government"* (London: Longman, Hurst, Rees, Orme, Brown & Green, 1825), cited in Banks, *Feminism and Family Planning*, p. 19.
41. Thomas Gisborne, *An Inquiry into the Duties of the Female Sex*, 7th ed. (London: T. Cadell and W. Davies, 1801), p. 12.
42. Ray Strachey, *"The Cause": A Short History of the Women's Movement in Great Britain* (London: G. Bell & Sons, 1928), p. 16.
43. Barbara Welter, "The Cult of True Womanhood: 1820-1860," *American Quarterly* 18 (1966): 152.
44. *Ladies Companion* 13 (1840): 113.
45. Welter, "Cult of True Womanhood," p. 154.
46. Langdon-Davies, *Short History of Women*, p. 347.
47. Banks, *Feminism and Family Planning*, p. 126.
48. Wollstonecraft, *Vindiction*, p. 150.
49. Ibid., p. 152.
50. Roberts, *Memoirs of Hannah More*, 1:427.
51. C. Willett Cunnington, *Feminine Attitudes in the Nineteenth Century* (New York: Macmillan Co., 1936), p. 70.
52. Quoted in George Catlin, Introduction to *Vindication*, by Wollstonecraft, p. xx.
53. Maurice J. Quinlan, *The Victorian Prelude: A History of English Manners, 1700-1830* (New York: Columbia University Press, 1941), p. 152.
54. Cunnington, *Feminine Attitudes*, p. 90.
55. Quoted in Hamilton, *England*, p. 332.
56. Ibid., p. 333.
57. Maria Edgeworth, *Practical Education*, 2 vols. (New York: Self, Brown & Stansbury, 1801), 2:550.
58. *Sentimental Magazine* 1 (July 1773): 209-10, quoted in Quinlan, *Victorian Prelude*, pp. 62-63.
59. An interesting and somewhat pathetic account of Hannah More's thrice-broken engagement appears in Mary Gwladys Jones, *Hannah More* (Cambridge: At the University Press, 1952), pp. 16ff, and in Mary Alden Hopkins, *Hannah More and Her*

Circle (New York: Longmans, Green & Co., 1947), pp. 32-37.

60. *Meliora: A Quarterly Review of Social Sciences, 1859-69* 2 (London, 1868):100.

61. Quoted in Strachey, *"The Cause"*, p. 16.

62. Alexander Walker, *Women Physiologically Considered as to Mind, Morals, Marriage, Matrimonial Slavery, Infidelity, and Divorce* (1839; reprint ed., Hartford, Conn.: Andrus, 1854), pp. 267-68.

63. The Property Act of 1870 represented a victory, albeit a small one, for women. It stated "that a woman might keep possession of what she earned, but all real property and personal property in excess of £200 was to belong to her husband." This right, too, is contradictory. Virtually no working-class woman could afford divorce, and very few middle-class women worked. The year 1872, however, saw a major development. The 1870 Act was amended, and "women gained full ownership of all property belonging to them at marriage or coming to them thereafter." Other rights were also slow in coming. In 1868 women were permitted to vote in municipal elections, and in 1888 in county councils. In 1918 women thirty years of age and over whose husbands owned or occupied land could vote. This ruling was still discriminatory, however, not only against younger women in general but against poor women in particular. Finally, in 1928, in the so-called flapper franchise, the vote was given to all women aged twenty-one years or over.

64. Mona Wilson, *These Were Muses* (London: Sidgwick, 1924), p. 82.

2
To Scrub the Floor or Dance upon It: The Rewards of Education

I would rather encounter a nest of wasps than a clever woman.[1]
— Mr. Headley, in *Marriage,*
a Novel

Nineteenth-century writings on women by women took their cue from the values of society. Much of what we think of today as the shortcomings of women's status in the early nineteenth century — second-class education, fixed roles, and the like — was actually reinforced by women themselves, particularly by women writers. The varieties of nonfiction written by women, mostly for women, included general works stressing women's role; studies of, and opinions on, women's education (even their teachers were women, for men, in a society that frowned on women's education, would not instruct them); religious and moral works; advice for the rearing of children, as well as stories for children; and personal diaries and journals. As various as all these readings seem, they were, nevertheless, similar in a number of respects. Didacticism, moralism, religiosity, and class consciousness are pervasive. "Piety, purity, submission, and domesticity," the four "cardinal virtues" of which Barbara Welter speaks, provided the model for the predominant nineteenth-century conception of the perfect woman, and nearly all of the women's literature conformed, even succumbed, to it. Clearly literature and life reinforced each other in the early nineteenth century.

No discussion of nineteenth-century nonfiction dealing with women would be complete without a treatment of Hannah More's life, work and attitudes. As the most prolific female writer of nonfiction of the last quarter of the eighteenth century and the first quarter of the nineteenth (she was born in 1745 and died in 1833), she was continually reinforcing women's subordinate role.

"She would have made a great man," said Byron about Madame de Stael.[2] This sentiment also applies to Hannah More. Although it was difficult for a woman to be emancipated in a man's world, in her work, More, like other women writers of the period, was often more reactive against women than supportive or innovative.

Hannah More, whose works were said to be, during the nineteenth century, better known in America than the plays of Shakespeare, tended to set herself above women, often even above humankind. She was a kind of self-appointed messiah. One of her biographers tells us that More carried on an imaginary correspondence "with depraved characters to reclaim them from their errors." The answers, also provided by More, "expressed their repentance and resolution of amendment."[3] Another biographer gives further evidence of Hannah More's messianic impulse, for in her later years, she tells us, More was most enthralled by visiting people on their deathbeds.[4]

Despite Hannah More's extraordinary sense of self, she came from an average upper-middle-class family. Her father, like the fathers of Anna L. Barbauld, Fanny Burney, and several other women writers, was a teacher. More and her four sisters were, like Barbauld, destined to teach as well as to write. Because Hannah More's father was a schoolmaster and because the classrooms of the More sisters were at home, one writer suggests that the family "looked upon the whole world as one great schoolhouse, upon human beings as willful pupils who would not learn their lessons, and upon themselves as ordained teachers."[5]

More's *Strictures on the Modern System of Female Education* (1799); *Coelebs in Search of a Wife* (1809), her only novel and undistinguishable from her nonfiction; *Practical Piety* (1811); *Christian Morals* (1812); and *Essays on the Character of St. Paul* (1815), all Christian oriented, naturally stress submissiveness. But they differ from standard Christian books, which defer to the Almighty; here, the author often sees herself as God. While her readers, at her behest, prayed submissively, More led an independent life, writing secular books and several plays. One of the latter, *Percy* (1777), a tragedy about royalty, was so successful that it earned her seven hundred pounds, an impressive sum at the time. Another play, *The Fatal Falsehood,* created a modest newspaper controversy when Hannah Parkhouse Cowley accused More of plagiarism. All of her plays were produced, because David Garrick, the famous Drury Lane actor, was a close friend. Besides him, More had many other male friends, including Samuel Johnson. Apparently, the wives of such luminaries did not interest Hannah; in fact, according to biographers, her few female friends were either widows or elderly spinsters.

While Hannah More preached piety for all women and perhaps practiced it herself to some degree, she still had the time and energy to lead a stimulating social and intellectual life. She was often in the company of the bright, the gregarious, the famous, and the wealthy. Evidently, she was eager to keep women in their place as long as she was not required to share it. She confessed in her diary (1776) that nothing on earth could be "more agreeable to my taste than my present manner of living," and she explained: "I am so much

Hannah More
COURTESY OF THE NATIONAL PORTRAIT GALLERY, LONDON

at my ease; have a great many hours at my disposal, to read my own books and see my own friends; and, whenever I please, may join the most polished and delightful society in the world."[6]

What is more to the point, she unequivocally subscribed to the male view of women. Speaking of a gathering of women to a friend (August 9, 1778), for instance, she complained that "the *ladies*, with loud vociferation seemed to *talk* much without *thinking* at all."[7] In her writings, moreover, she vehemently and consistently downgrades woman's intelligence. In *Strictures*, she asserts that women were unable to integrate knowledge. "What knowledge they have. . .stands out as if it were above the very surface of their minds, like the *applique* of the embroiderer instead of having been interwoven with the growth of the piece, so as to have become a part of the stuff."[8] In short, she believed, women paraded rather than integrated knowledge.

But when she stresses that women's education should prepare them to be "daughters, wives, mothers, and mistresses of families" (in contrast to education for men who, she states, "are commonly destined. . .[for] some profession"), it is no wonder that women were "unable to integrate knowledge."[9]

More was even against women's being trained in the arts, a practice that most women's schools in the nineteenth century stressed in view of society's strong opposition to anything more intellectual. "In all polished countries," she writes, without substantiation, "an entire devotedness to the fine arts has become one grand source of the corruption of women."[10]

An underlying and disturbing illogic is apparent in many of her views. For example, having reduced women to mere robots who pray, keep house, and bear children, she goes on to contend that woman's "impatience, levity, and fickleness. . .are perhaps in no small degree aggravated by the littleness and frivolousness of female pursuits. The sort of education they commonly receive, teaches girls to set a great price on small things."[11]

Another glaring instance of her illogic involves her accusation that woman is vain, and that her interest in clothes and beauty often makes her immoral. In what is clearly a grossly biased oversimplification, Hannah More says that "women who are ruined by seduction in the lower classes, and those who are made miserable by ambitious marriages in the higher, will be more frequently found to owe their misery to an ungoverned passion for dress and show."[12] But she misses the mark. Girls who were denied knowledge and culture, who were taught that fulfillment is possible only through marriage, would inevitably and understandably pursue one goal: a husband.

The financial and social independence that More enjoyed, she earnestly tried, however inadvertently, to prevent other women from achieving. Edward Turner, Hannah More's former fiancé, left her a legacy of one thousand pounds and settled an annuity on her of two hundred pounds a year. Furthermore, the girls' boarding school that she and her sisters had founded in Bristol was very profitable, and after thirty years they sold it for a sizable sum. But Hannah More was not the only unconscious enemy of her own sex. Other women writers were also antifeminist — in effect if not by design. Both Ann Taylor and Jane West, although less prolific than Hannah More, shared her general views on women.

Ann Taylor (1782-1866) and her younger sister, Jane, were educated at home by their father, a minister. Their mother was a practical woman who supervised her daughters' domestic learning (needlepoint, flower arranging) as well as their religious education. The Taylor household was large and the children had a great deal of space and materials. Ann and Jane were both unusually bright and imaginative, and during the first few years of their lives they could read, sing, recite, and write. They wrote mostly for each other, but this writing was not encouraged by their parents, who were more interested in preparing their children for the "discharge of the ordinary duties of life."[13]

Although both sisters wrote poetry, novels, and nonfiction,

Ann and Jane Taylor
COURTESY OF THE NATIONAL PORTRAIT GALLERY, LONDON

each was apologetic about her and her sister's labors. Jane said that Ann wrote neither for gain nor for admiration, but only for amusement, and Ann said that Jane "was fond of the labours of the needle and of every domestic engagement." She proudly stated that her sister was "free. . .from that ambition which often accompanies intellectual superiority," and added: "To the character of a *literary lady* she had, in fact, a decided dislike."[14]

Jane never married, and she died at the age of forty-one. Ann married a minister and raised a large family. After her marriage she wrote a few religious books for children and a memoir of her husband.

In *Practical Hints to Young Females on the Duties of a Wife, a Mother, and a Mistress of a Family*, Ann Taylor clearly outlines what she thought was the best and possibly only goal for a woman—marriage. Ironically, her sympathies are directed toward the husband, for, like almost all nineteenth-century women, Taylor, by inference, believed that men are superior. When a man marries, she says, he stakes "the happiness of his future life."[15] Unfortunately, she is unconcerned about woman's marital commitment. "There cannot. . .be a sight more uncouth, than that of a man and his wife struggling for power," she goes on, "for where it ought to be vested, nature, reason, and scripture, concur to declare."[16] Her position is like that of Hannah More, who explains in *Moral Sketches* that "competition and emulation [in marriage] do not contain the elements of domestic happiness."[17]

Practical Hints was mainly addressed to "females in the middle ranks of society," to women who ought to be married as quickly as possible, according to Ann Taylor. She laments the fact that the middle-class woman was often duped by her education. "Many a female. . .returns home [from boarding school] not to assist her mother, but to support her [own] pretensions to gentility by idleness, dress and dissipation," Taylor argues; and she adds: "She concludes herself degraded by domestic occupation."[18] The difference between the lower- and upper-middle classes is made quite clear. While upper-middle-class women were tied to their homes, but not to housework, lower-middle-class women were expected fully to engage in "domestic occupation" and to work as diligently in their homes as their husbands did out of them.

In view of Ann Taylor's position, most of her book is appropriately devoted to domestic matters. Pay bills weekly, buy in quantity, keep servants in their place, "supervise them well," and encourage religious principles and high morals in the home — these are the foci. Every kitchen should house a library of appropriate works — for example, Hannah More's *Cheap Repository* — because "the lessons there given, and the examples exhibited," Ann Taylor says, "judiciously blend amusement with instruction."[19]

Jane West (1758-1852), who was friendly with both Ann and Jane Taylor, was entirely self-educated and began writing verse at thirteen. Little is known about her early childhood, but she married a farmer and had several children. Besides supervising the household and dairy, she wrote novels, poems, plays, and educational tracts, many of which were published anonymously during her lifetime.

Jane West, in both *The Advantages of Education* and *Letters to a Young Lady, in Which the Duties and Characters of Women are Considered, Chiefly with a Reference to Prevailing Opinions*, stresses, in a like manner, the importance of marriage, as well as the superiority of the male. Here, marriage is "a heaven-ordained bond, . . .[a] sacred source of all domestic relations and charities."[20] In marriage, women "enter upon the most extended circle in which. . .Providence designed us to move."[21] Moreover, in Letter 12, "On Celibacy, Love, and Marriage," she judiciously debates "the most eligible [state] for women, the single or the married" life.[22] Following prevailing opinion, she concludes that the latter is superior, for "certainly, the condition which the Almighty created us to occupy must be most conducive to our general happiness."[23] It is interesting how often Christian dogma is invoked — actually exploited — to keep woman in her place.

Besides insisting that marriage is right for women because God believes in and ordained marriage, West amplifies her proposition by citing social practice. Women "are far less able than men to be the carvers of [their] fortunes," she argues, and "must generally consult *more* than [their]. . .own inclinations in order to be happy."[24] Not unexpectedly, then, she concludes that "to superintend and conduct a household with regularity, propriety, elegance, and good humour, is a happy art."[25]

Finally, in another rationalization for keeping woman in the home, West explains that "improved capacity always implies increased responsibility; knowledge is a most precious talent and must pay the highest price."[26] Perhaps to lessen the blow that she delivers to her sex, West adds that "consciousness of ignorance is a degree of knowledge."[27] Indeed, "a bright imagination, a glow of generous sentiment and polished and correct expression," claims West, "are all parts of the character of an accomplished female; diversity of idea and playful allusion, also claim admission into this charming group of sister graces."[28] Clearly, women, especially spokeswomen who wrote, were often their own severest enemies.

The only way women — or any oppressed group, for that matter — could gain equality before and during the early nineteenth century was through education. Young upper-class men had been receiving excellent educations for at least two hundred years. As we know from reading the biographies of such writers as Milton and Dryden, boys were taught several languages, ancient as well as modern, and science and philosophy, among other subjects. Not only was their education academic; it also took into account their physical wellbeing. In *Thoughts Concerning Education* (1693), John Locke devotes a considerable section to the Juvenalian principle of a "sound mind in a sound body," and stresses nutrition and exercise.

However, on the subject of education for females Locke was somewhat sketchy. In fact, his only comment appears in a letter written in 1685 to a mother who, surprisingly, was concerned about her daughter's education as well as her son's. Locke answered: "There will be some though no great difference, for making a little allowance for beauty and some few other considerations of the s[ex], [but] the manner of breeding of boys and girls, especially in their younger years, I imagine should be the same."[29]

Practically the only time that child education of both sexes was the same was during the preschool years, extending to age five or six. Even among the lower classes there was a marked distinction in the degree of education for boys and for girls. Many young boys of the working classes were, unlike their sisters, taught how to read and write. In fact, they were even taught Latin, though not so extensively as were boys of the upper class. But, most significantly, they were taught a trade—usually by way of apprenticeship—so that they would eventually be able to earn a living. On the other hand, education for middle- and upper-class girls, as described by William Gifford in his piece on *The Daughters of Isenberg* in the *Quarterly Review*, consisted of "a little French, a little music, a little botany, a little conchology—in short, a little of everything."[30] The emphasis here is on *little*. Indeed, the prevailing view of women's education can be summed up with Rousseau's comment from *Émile; or, Education* (1782): "Woman was made especially to please man" for she "is formed to...live in subjection";[31] consequently, he implies, education would be wasted on her.

In the cacophony of outcries against women as people, there were a few lonely voices that asserted that women could be, through education, more fulfilled, even equal to men, and that they should be given the chance. Significantly, two writers who championed a more complete education for women were men, one a Frenchman.

Paul Henri d'Holbach recognized the importance of education for women, for in "On Women" in his *Système social*

(1773) he denounces man's tyrannical treatment of the sex. Moreover, in his report on national education, *Sur l' instruction publique*, which he prepared for the French Revolutionary Convention in 1792, he maintains not only that the system of national education should "be the same for women as for men" but also that "men [will not] retain their intellectual interests unless they can share them with women." "Women," he states, "have the same natural right to knowledge and enlightenment as men,"[32] and he implies that men are also the beneficiaries of this educational equality — a modern notion indeed.

Thomas Broadhurst shared Holbach's viewpoint, and in his eight-volume work, *Advice to Young Ladies on the Improvement of the Mind*, he acknowledges the general opposition to the education of women, provides a brief history of women's education, and stresses its importance. According to Broadhurst, the primary reason for depriving women of the education men receive is that women have more "idle time." Whereas men are physicians, lawyers, apothecaries, and so on, women take care of children and pay bills, he says, a somewhat procrustean attitude that raises a question about Broadhurst's sincerity.

Broadhurst cites another reason why society deprives females of a proper education: "Educated women become affected and conceited." But he modifies his position by observing that "vanity and conceit. . .[can be] witness[ed] in [both] men and women." "When learning ceases to be uncommon among women, learned women will cease to be affected."[33] Finally, Broadhurst candidly admits that "it is natural that men who are ignorant themselves, should view with some degree of jealousy and alarm, any proposal for improving the education of women."[34] His insight is not unimpressive.

Broadhurst, however, guardedly qualifies his egalitarian suggestions. A woman's education is, in the main, for private, not for public use. "A woman should be able to use her knowledge for her private happiness, her own contentment," says Broadhurst, and, like Hannah More, he condemns an education that focuses exclusively on fine arts—drawing, painting, and music. "A century past, women's education stressed housewifery,—now it is for [artistic] accomplishments."[35] He continues with a statement reminiscent of Mary Wollstonecraft's argument in *Vindication:* "The system of female education as it now stands, aims at embellishing a few years of life, which are in themselves so full of grace and happiness, that they hardly want it; and leave the rest of existence a miserable prey to idle insignificance."[36] Thus, says Broadhurst, for women the loss of youth is the loss of "all," and "every human being must put up with the coldest civility, who has neither the charms of youth nor the wisdom of age."[37]

Broadhurst's views were advanced—he did some essential ground-clearing—but his work never fulfilled its intention. It proposed a different, a better and more equal, education for women. But it did not go beyond the goal of personal fulfillment. Women were still trapped in their homes.

Essentially, the term *education*, when applied to women, was a euphemism for something else. Writers like Hannah More, Anna L. Barbauld, and Jane West were concerned mainly with the correctness of women's social behavior and with their roles as wives and mothers. In addition, the class consciousness that pervaded all of English society, including women, strongly influenced women's education, which was, fundamentally, preparation for socially defined roles. The idea of constraining each class of women was, in general, strictly proselytized by the writers on women's education. For example, Jane West states in *Letters* that "it is [her] wish to warn young women from aiming at conquests, on the score of their personal attraction, to which neither their birth, connections, education, nor situation entitle them to aspire."[38]

While nearly all the women writing on education came from the upper-middle class, they took the liberty of writing for and about other classes. For instance, Elizabeth Hamilton was concerned exclusively with the upper class, Jane West and Ann Taylor were concerned with the middle and upper classes, and Frances Broadhurst, wife of Thomas, devoted her writing and her efforts (she ran a boarding school) to the newly moneyed agricultural and industrial classes. Anna L. Barbauld was concerned with the upper middle classes and Mary Wollstonecraft with the lower middle classes. Significantly, Hannah More, who produced more books on education than all of these women combined, wrote on the eduation of all three classes. It was she, in fact, who helped to initiate the Sunday school movement, the first system of education for the lower class, which will be discussed later.

Hannah More's three books on education for the upper class, which were enthusiastically received, included *Strictures on the Modern System of Female Education with a View to the Principles and Conduct of Women of Rank and Fortune*, which was published in 1799 and went through thirteen editions—a total of nineteen thousand copies. Considering the limited number of readers in those days, as well as men's lack of interest in female education, this was a phenomenal achievement. Obviously the upper-middle-class woman, confined to her home but with nothing to do in it, literally devoured any acceptable reading material. Moreover, most of the literary periodicals, such as the *Monthly Mirror*, praised the work highly, since it did advocate keeping women in their place. *Hints for Forming the Character of a Princess* (1805) had a very limited appeal, since it was written for Princess Charlotte of Wales after the Bishop of London decided to entrust the Princess's education to More. The plan failed to materialize—the Princess died in 1814—but Hannah More did educate Lord Thomas Babington Macaulay during his early years, and he always remained grateful. *Coelebs in Search of a Wife* (1809), a novel that offers more opinions on the education of women than does More's nonfictional works, went through twelve editions and earned two thousand pounds — all within a single year.

The theme of *Strictures* is that "while men must be educated, women should be trained."[39] The text is essentially negative, concentrating, as it does, on what women should not do rather than on what they should. Hannah More was opposed to women's using their physical attractions to achieve any gains. Like Elizabeth Hamilton, she believed that this would cause the class system to disintegrate. Furthermore, More believed that if women earned admiration and attention solely for their looks, they would not want to remain unseen at home, would not want to be dutiful wives and mothers. Thus she deplored educating women for "crowds," when they spend most of their time at home, for "the world," rather than for "themselves," for "show," not for "use," for "time" and not for "eternity."[40] She therefore warns mothers that their daughters should "not be intoxicated by the praise of the world," and she stresses "the shortness and uncertainty of beauty."[41] Here Hannah More seems to be echoing Rousseau, who states in *Émile* that woman's "honour consists in being unknown, her glory in the esteem of her husband, her pleasure in the happiness of her family."[42]

As was mentioned earlier, Hannah More also discouraged women's being educated in the arts. In *Strictures* she describes the characteristics of the marriageable woman. "When a man of sense comes to marry, it is a companion whom he wants," she asserts, "and not an artist. It is not merely a creature who can paint, play and sing and draw and dress and dance; it is a being who can comfort and counsel him; one who can reason and reflect and feel and judge, and discourse and discriminate; one who can assist him in his affairs, lighten his cares, sooth[e] his sorrows, purify his joys, strengthen his principles and educate his children."[43]

In *Coelebs*, Hannah More describes the educated woman, or, more accurately, the perfect wife. Coelebs's mother, who speaks for Hannah More, says: " 'I call education not that which is made up of the shreds and patches of useless arts, but that which inculcates principles, polishes taste, regulates temper. cultivates reason, subdues the passions. directs the feelings, habituates the reflection, trains to self-denial, and, more especially, that which refers all actions, feelings, sentiments, tastes, and passions, to the love and fear of God.' "[44] Actually, Hannah More's definition is neither all negative nor all traditional. The problem is, how does a woman become reasonable and reflective if she is not formally trained? In a section on the forming of habits in *Strictures*, More praises the typical Christian virtues of "humility," "sobriety," "meekness," "attention," and "industry." Thus we come full circle—from Welter's cardinal virtues and back.

But Hannah More did not always practice what she advocated. The opening in Bristol, of Mores' Boarding School, founded by Hannah and her four sisters, took place in March 1758. The announcement in the Bristol newspaper said that "French, Reading, Writing, Arithmetic and needlework [will] be carefully taught." It was repeated the following week with this further information: "A dancing master will properly attend."[45] Thus the Mores, conceivably placing money before precept, probably capitulated to public demand.

Whereas Hannah More believed in boarding schools for the education of middle- and upper-class women, most women writers who wrote on the subject of the eduction of the upper classes favored mothers and governesses as teachers, perhaps in emulation of upper-class male students, who had male tutors. Individualized instruction was, apparently, more genteel. Elizabeth Hamilton, in her *Letters on the Elementary Principles of Education*, designed for upper-class women, offers some original theories but does not really discuss the principles and practices of education. In contrast to her rather conventional preface, in which she claims that she had written her "little book" on education "not to criticize the systems of others, nor to offer mechanical rules for facilitating the work of

Elizabeth Hamilton
COURTESY OF THE NATIONAL PORTRAIT GALLERY, LONDON

instruction, but humbly to throw in my quota of observation and experience, as a small addition to the general stock," she boldly analyzes the prejudice that men are superior to women. The idea of male superiority, she says, "evidently originated [in primitive times] for in the savage state bodily strength gives an indisputable title to superiority."[46]

Without explicitly stating that women are superior to men in educating their children, Hamilton claims in an unsupported assertion that "the degeneracy of morals under the [Roman] emperors is. . .traced to the period when mothers began to give up the eduction of their children to slaves and hirelings."[47] She believed, then, that mothers must educate their daughters. In *Thoughts on the Education of Daughters*, Mary Wollstonecraft, too, believed that young ladies should be instructed at home, but not merely for the purpose of occupying the time of otherwise idle mothers. She deplored the superficiality of boarding schools and their lack of real learning. Several years later, however, in *Vindication*, Mary Wollstonecraft discusses the "perfect" school—one with no class distinctions (as evidenced in dress, for example,), with recreation as well as sedentary pursuits, and with a wide range of courses such as botany, mechanics, philosophy, and astronomy. Above all, she advises that boys and girls attend classes together.

Apparently, some women writers were aware of the shortcomings of contemporary female education, but they seemed to focus on particulars, often minute, rather than on the overall discrimination and segregation of the sexes that was practiced in early-nineteenth-century England.

For example, Elizabeth Hamilton criticized female education in that "no one power of the mind is called into exercise, except memory." She also condemned education that was "thrust upon children." Learning should be gradual, and students should be motivated. But aside from these few perfunctory comments on methods of teaching, she concentrated mainly on the "cardinal virtues" of women.

"Hostility" and "timidity" are detriments to learning; instead, Hamilton prefers "humility" and "diffidence." She advocates kindliness toward servants, while keeping them in their place. A large part of volume 1 is devoted to religion, its general importance, and its influence upon us.

Like Thomas Broadhurst in his eight volumes of opinions on women's education, Hamilton claims that in order for a mother to be truly respectable in the eyes of her offspring, she must be capable of instructing them. But Hamilton says nothing about women's instructing others or preparing for professions.

Jane West's *The Advantages of Education; or, The History of Maria Williams* (1803) is a didactic novel, but her *Letters to a Young Lady, in Which the Duties and Character of Women are Considered* (1806) was written in epistolary form to the daughter of the author's deceased friend. It attempts to make women satisfied, even elated, with their current role by describing how bad things were in the past. For example, the author offers a brief history of women, explaining that in barbaric societies women were "depressed, servile, and miserable."

Whereas Hannah More had deplored women's being educated in the arts, Jane West urges women's exposure to cultural pursuits, but only superficially. She suggests that "drawing and music. . .[though] most pleasing accomplishments and agreeable methods of employing leisure, may be so far pursued, as to prove a serious consumpion of time and fortune." She recommends "cards [which] when accompanied by vivacity and good humour, afford relief to the flagging conversation."[48] In stark contrast, Mary Wollstonecraft claims that card playing "calls forth the most unpleasing passions." Wollstonecraft adds that "cards are the universal refuge to which the idle and the ignorant resort, to pass life away."[49]

But, denied knowledge, what were women to do? If "they stole knowledge, they must learn like the Spartan youths, to

hide their furtive gains," advised Anna L. Barbauld (whose
texts for children will be discussed in the next chapter). They
"must be content to know that a thing is so without understanding the proof, [for] the thefts of knowledge in our sex are
only connived at while carefully concealed, and if displayed
punished with disgrace."[50]

When women were shielded from real learning at home, and
when most boarding schools' curricula were frivolous, they
found themselves without knowledge — and therefore unable to
conceal it. In "A Word in Favour of Female Schools: Addressed to Parents and Guardians and the Public at large" in the
Pamphleteer, Francis Broadhurst, who for thirty years ran a
school for young middle-class ladies, discusses the advantages
of a "formal school education" over the shortcomings related to
children's being taught at home by mothers and governesses.[51]
For one thing, governesses, she maintains, are never truly
dedicated to strangers; it is implied, of course, that her
teachers, strangers too, *are*. Typically, Broadhurst discusses
what she claims to be the greatest single advantage in a school
education — "order" and "respectability." She asserts that she
remained with her pupils at all times to inculcate these virtues,
and that her female teachers, "besides their own individual
merit, were of respectable families." However, Broadhurst
never discusses curriculum, career-orientation, or the
educative process — just behavior patterns, "order," and
"respectability."

Again, Mary Wollstonecraft sounded the lone voice of
feminine protest — this time against women's education, or,
more precisely, the lack of it. In *Thoughts on the Education of
Daughters*, she contradicts Broadhurst's views on boarding
schools, and advocates the instruction of young ladies in the
home. She condemns the emphasis placed on manners at
boarding schools, and argues that "few things are learnt
thoroughly."[52] She encourages wide reading and stresses the
"importance of the mind to develop inner resources so as not to
be dependent on the senses for employment and

amusement."[53] She belittles women's "trifling conversations [that are] prone to ridicule" and the inordinate amount of time spent on clothes. "Dress," she states, "ought to adorn the person and not rival it."[54] Knowledge and developing one's intelligence are of primary importance. "In a comfortable situation," she explains, "a cultivated mind is necessary to render a woman contented; and in a miserable one, it is her only consolation."[55]

In the most poignant chapter of all, Mary Wollstonecraft reveals her own plight, the "unfortunate situation of [middleclass] females, fashionably educated, and left without a fortune." She enumerates the "humiliating" jobs available to such women: as companions to tedious old women, as school teachers who work harder than menial servants, and as governesses to young ladies.

If women were to have professions at all, according to the general view, they should be Christian missionaires, a point that Hannah More makes in *Strictures*, where she urges women "to raise the depressed tone of public morals and to awaken the drowsy spirit of religious principles." Even Mary Wollstonecraft claims in *Thoughts on the Education of Daughters* that "the main business in our lives is to learn to be virtuous," "never [to] despair, to trust in God."

While upper-class females were, for the most part, educated at home, and middle-class women were sent to boarding schools, the lower, or working class received their education in Sunday schools. Actually, Sunday schools grew out of the Evangelical movement, the Evangelicals being a Protestant sect emphasizing the authority of the Gospel, and holding that salvation results from faith and grace rather than from good works and sacraments alone. The movement was essentially "an effort to rouse the Church of England from the somewhat lethargic state into which it had fallen."[56] Hannah More belonged to the Clapham Sect of Evangelicals, Protestants who were often more concerned with practical morality and philanthropy than with theology. The large number of religious works that she published, in addition to her participation in the Sunday school movement, caused her to be referred to as "one of the 'great men' of the [Evangelical] party."[57]

More, along with the others in the movement, began to open Sunday schools in working-class neighborhoods. The Mores faced much opposition in getting these schools organized. Parents were hostile to the idea of relieving their children of household and other work in order to attend. In a letter to a friend, Hannah describes the difficulties she encountered in Cheddar. Every house, she reported, was "a scene of the greatest ignorance and vice. We saw but one Bible in all the parish, and that was used to prop a flower pot."[58] However, after the first schools were established, for the people of Cheddar, they quickly sprang up throughout industrial Britain.

In addition to pressuring employers and to "scolding" mothers, the Mores relied on a system of small rewards to motivate their students. For example, a penny was given to each child for punctuality for four successive Sundays. Bibles, prayerbooks, tracts, and even clothing, were distributed once a year according to merit.

The schools sought to instill religious principles, that is, good conduct, cleanliness, and honesty, but they also taught reading and writing. These Bible schools were frequently associated with schools of industry, where girls were taught spinning, weaving, knitting, sewing, cooking, and other skills needed at home or in domestic service.

As for the curriculum, More wrote some of her own textbooks, such as *Questions and Answers for the Mendip Schools.* The main reliance was on the Old and the New Testaments, the Psalter, the Book of Common Prayer, and spelling books. Parables were used as "groundwork in teaching."[59]

More personally engaged the instructresses, as well as mistresses to teach spinning. Not only did the schools prepare the girls exclusively to be good wives and homemakers, but also More helped to reinforce women's second-class position within marriage by barring any married women from her staff. "A female teacher, regardless of her efficiency, was discharged when she married or even upon her betrothal."[60]

Still, the emphasis for all female students was on marriage. Any girl who continued to attend the school through her teens was rewarded with five shillings, a pair of white stockings, and a new Bible — on her wedding day. More even wrote a cookbook called *The Cottage Cook* to help wives get the most out of their limited supplies.

Other upper-middle-class women also became involved in the Sunday school movement. Mary Martha Butt Sherwood, whose *Journals* will be discussed in chapter 3, wrote about making bonnets for "our girls," walking them to church, and visiting them on weekdays. She seemed to take a more sincere interest in the girls themselves than did Hannah More. She was most concerned with their virtue — so that they would marry suitably — and she wrote *Susan Gray*, a religious and moralistic novel, for "the elder girls in [her] Sunday School," and she read it aloud to them chapter by chapter.

Jane West, while never actually teaching working-class girls, praises in her *Letters* a book by an anonymous author entitled *Lucy Franklin*. "It attacks that rage for finery which is so unhappily prevalent among young women in low life (and which mistresses of families *may* and *ought* to discourage)," she writes, "showing them that it is the most likely means to plunge them into all the miseries of disgrace and ruin."[61]

Nevertheless, with all the warnings from books and teachers, girls still managed to get into trouble, and Hannah More always tried to rescue them. The first was Clementina, a fourteen-year-old student in one of the Mores' schools, who had eloped with an older man who married her, promptly took possession of her inheritance, and left her. More intervened in vain. The girl, young and poverty-stricken, died, and the man prospered from his late wife's inheritance. This unfortunate situation never suggested to Hannah More, however, the need for a change in women's legal status. Indeed, when Mary Wollstonecraft's *Vindication of the Rights of Women* was published in the very same year that Clementina was seduced, Hannah More refused to read the book. Her comment was: "Rights of women! . . .How many ways are there of being ridiculous!"[62]

A second victim was a girl who tried to drown herself in the canal in St. James' Park, and a third, whom More supported for a while, was a crazy woman who lived in a haystack. A fourth, the most noteworthy, was Ann Yearsley, the milkwoman whom More, exerting exclusive control, tried to turn into a poetess. Ann Yearsley, living in poverty with her laborer husband and their six children, managed somehow to write a series of crude poems that came to More's attention. After helping Yearsley with her grammar and spelling, and editing her poems, More, along with her friend Elizabeth Montagu, published them. They also added "a condescending preface" and a list of the subscribers secured by Montagu, including Edward Turner, More's former fiancé.

Both Hannah More and Elizabeth Montagu were also patronizing in their attitude toward Ann Yearsley. For example, in a letter to More (1784), Montagu wrote: "Wonder not, therefore, if our humble dame rises above Pindar, or steps beyond Aeschylus." She sarcastically added: "Lactilla's [Ann Yearsley's] poems did not arive here till last night, and then by a conveyance that was most unworthy of a muse—a broad-wheeled stage wagon."[63]

The major break between Hannah More and Ann Yearsley came when More, with Elizabeth Montagu, sought to control the money that Yearsley's poems earned. Hannah had decided to apportion the money out a little at a time as she saw fit, for that would provide "an income sufficient for [the Yearsley family's] low social status."[64] A heated argument erupted between the two women, with nearly all the townspeople taking sides, but Yearsley refused to relent in her demands and eventually got all of her money.

To turn a working-class woman into a polished poet was a more difficult task than to turn a woman of any class into a religious paragon. Many of the women who wrote about women's education, which stressed piety, also wrote books on morals and religion. Although most critics of education agreed that women should be educated according to their social station, they believed that the religious education of the poor and of the rich had to inculcate the same principles. If women had to read at all, for instance, it was generally agreed that the subjects of religion and religious biography were best.

Women writers stressed the importance of religion itself; hence the necessity for women to spread the Gospel. "The dignity of the work to which you are called," Hannah More writes in *Strictures*, "is no less than that of preserving the Ark of the Lord."[65] Similarly, Jane West depicts religion as a woman's panacea. Quoting from the Bible, she writes in the frontispiece to *Letters:* "Favour is deceitful, and beauty is vain, but a woman that feareth the Lord, she shall be praised."[66] The entire last part of volume 2 of *Letters* is devoted to religion: "No minutias are undeserving of serious consideration, which contribute to the peace and goodwill of the little kingdom over which we exert viceregal dignity."[67]

Religious instruction for women was the be-all and end-all. Hannah More called it "our compass, the only instrument for directing and determining our course."[68] Elizabeth Hamilton wrote that: "when the judgement has been previously strengthened by religious principle, imagination will ever afterward submit to the control of reason."[69] Religion was the basis of women's education. Not only More and Hamilton, but Frances Broadhurst, Sarah Trimmer, and Maria Edgeworth all condemned making religion an abstract study. Religion was very real to them, and they unanimously recommended that women should study thoroughly the history of both the Old and the New Testaments. Finally, the study of religion was never-ending. Said Hannah More: "The noblest things are the longest in attaining their perfection . . .[and] there is no assignable period when our virtues will be incapable of addition."[70]

In the category of books on morals and religion, Hannah More led the list of women writers. Her *Moral Sketches of Prevailing Opinions and Manners, Foreign and Domestic: With Reflections on Prayer* (1819) sold very well. More was seventy-five when she wrote it, but her habit of didacticism and her conservative and usually negative opinions persisted. Topics covered in *Moral Sketches* are "the disobedience of children, the impudence of servants, the rebellion of labourers, the levity of society, the extravagance of the poor and the depravity of foreign lands."[71]

Her other religious works include *Practical Piety, Christian Morals*, and *Essays on the Character of St. Paul.* Even Hannah More was occasionally attacked by the male critics. In a review of *Christian Morals* that appeared in the *Monthly Review* (February 1813), the reviewer claimed that the work was "redundant" and "hypocritical." The last twenty pages or so of *Strictures* are devoted to religion. For several years Hannah had been rewriting Bible stories in dialogue. Eventually she put them into *Sacred Dramas* (1811), which was reprinted in nineteen editions. Her voluminous writing, coupled with her work in Sunday schools for the poor, caused More to lament to friends that she "spent more time working for God than in meditating upon Him."[72] For once, however, More practiced what she preached, for in *Strictures* she urges that "young ladies . . . set apart a fixed portion of their time, as sacred to the poor, whether in relieving, instructing, or working for them."[73]

Hannah More reached the middle and upper classes mainly through her writings, but she also opened Sunday schools, recruited students, taught many pupils, and, along with her sister Patty, established women's clubs patterned on men's friendly societies. More and her sister would preach at the clubs, warning the girls that "dancing led to dishonour," and telling children that if they came to Sunday school for tarts and clothing instead of from a sense of duty, God would punish them.

Hannah More's religious writings for the poor took several forms. She wrote religious tracts, which were bought in the thousands by the well-to-do and distributed to the poor. Tracts on morals and religion written by Hannah More and other female writers were so successful that male journalists exploited the situation and wrote tracts under female pseudonyms.

Equally popular among the lower classes were More's exemplary stories, one of which was about a young girl called "Sally of the Green" who became "sinful Sally" and later "drunken Sal" — until she finally came to "a Melancholy and almost Hopeless End." In all such tracts, the good are rewarded or taken to heaven, while the sinful repent, go to jail, or are hanged.

As C. Willett Cunnington aptly expresses it, "Morality, with scarcely a rag of disguise, stalks through the volumes, while Religion bludgeons a path that none can miss."[76] The chief criticism of these exemplary books — and of many novels as well — is that, while "such works had the obvious design of making their readers good," they did not make them "critical, for problems are never presented, but only stereotyped solutions."[75]

A third type of moralistic writing by Hannah More for the poor was political ballads. Implicit in them was the prevailing middle- and upper-class idea that rigid social distinction was fundamental to God's own benevolent plan, and that it was therefore wrong for the poor to attempt to improve their economic or social position by means of workers' unions or through efforts to change discriminatory laws.

Moreover, Hannah More "could not believe, . . .that the poor would benefit from parliamentary reform. . . .The duty of charity *to* the poor, the duty of acquiescence *by* the poor, defined her social philosophy."[76]

The following ballad,[77] taught to the discontented working-class poor, was reported to have stopped a riot near Bath.

But though poor, I can work, my brave boy, with the best,

Let the king and the parliament manage the rest;
I lament both the war and the taxes together,
Though I verily think they don't alter the weather.
The king as I take it, with very good reason,
May prevent a bad law, but can't help a bad season.
                              Derry down.

And though I've no money, and though I've no lands;
I've a head on my shoulders, and a pair of good hands;
So I'll work the whole day, and on Sundays I'll seek
At church how to bear all the wants of the weak.
The gentlefolks too will afford us supplies,
They'll subscribe—and they'll give up their pudding and
pies.
                              Derry down.

Then before I'm induced to take part in a riot,
I'll ask this short question—What shall I get by it?
So I'll e'en wait a little, till cheaper the bread,
For a mittimus hangs o'er each rioter's head;
And when of two evils I'm asked which is best
I'd rather be hungry than hang'd I protest.
                              Derry down.

Other women besides Hannah More wrote on morals and
religion, but much of their writing has failed to survive. More's
work, moreover, was not only representative of women's early
nineteenth-century nonfiction, but it was also quite extensive.
Nevertheless, men preferred to underestimate or simply to ignore female writers. The following anecdote was typical.

When Boswell told Dr. Johnson of a Quaker lady whom he
heard preach, Johnson commented: "Sir, a woman's preaching
is like a dog's walking on his hind legs. It is not done well; but
you are surprised to find it done at all!"[78] Yet women writers
continued to preach, even though their sermons were delivered
in pages of their books rather than in pulpits, and mainly to
other women. In succeeding chapters, where other forms of
nonfiction are discussed—children's stories and journals, as
well as novels—it will become evident that writing by women

was not only "done," but "done well," and that it had a considerable impact.

NOTES

1. Mr. Headley, in Susan Ferrier, *Marriage, a Novel*, ed. Herbert Foltinek (1818; reprint ed., London: Oxford University Press, 1971), p. 439.

2. Catherine J. Hamilton, *Women Writers: Their Works and Ways*, 1st ser. (1892; reprint ed., New York: Books for Libraries Press, 1971), p. 65.

3. Ibid., p. 83.

4. Mary Alden Hopkins, *Hannah More and Her Circle* (New York: Longmans, Green & Co., 1947), p. 199.

5. Ibid., p. 13.

6. Hannah More, *Memoirs of the Life and Correspondence of Mrs. Hannah More*, ed. William Roberts, 2 vols. (New York: Harper & Bros., 1837), 1:53.

7. Ibid., p. 88.

8. Hannah More, *Strictures on the Modern System of Female Education with a View to the Principles and Conduct of Women of Rank and Fortune, The Works of Hannah More*, 11 vols. (London: T. Cadell, 1830), 5:372.

9. Ibid., p. 329.

10. Ibid., p. 325.

11. Ibid., p. 381.

12. Ibid., p. 336.

13. Isaac Taylor, *Memoirs and Political Remains of the Late Jane Taylor with Extracts from Her Correspondence* (Philadelphia, Pa.: J. J. Woodward, 1827), p. 15.

14. Ibid., p. 140.

15. Ann Taylor, *Practical Hints to Young Females on the Duties of a Wife, A Mother, and a Mistress of a Family*, 3d ed. (London: Taylor & Hessey, 1815), p. 11.

16. Ibid., p. 14.

17. Hannah More, *Moral Sketches of Prevailing Opinions and Manners, Foreign and Domestic: With Reflections on Prayer, The Works of Hannah More*, 11 vols. (London: T. Cadell, 1830), 4:35.

18. Ann Taylor, *Practical Hints*, p. 3.

19. Ibid., p. 41.

20. Jane West, *Letters to a Young Lady in Which the Duties and Character of Women Are Considered, Chiefly with a Reference to Prevailing Opinions*. 4th ed. 3 vols. (London: Longman, Hurst, Rees, Orme & Brown, 1811), 1:40.

21. Ibid., p. 45.

22. Ibid., 3:87.

23. Ibid.

24. Ibid., 1:67.

25. Ibid., p. 77.

26. Ibid., 3:6.
27. Ibid., pp. 6-7.
28. Ibid., 2:467.
29. John Locke, *The Educational Writings of John Locke*, ed. James L. Axtell (Cambridge: At the University Press, 1968), p. 5.
30. *Quarterly Review* 4 (August 1810):61.
31. Jean Jacques Rousseau, *Émile; or, Education*, trans. Barbara Foxley (1762; reprint ed., New York: E. P. Dutton & Co., 1911), p. 322.
32. Paul Henri d'Holbach, *Système social* (Amsterdam: Londres, 1773) p. 122.
33. Thomas Broadhurst, *Advice to Young Ladies on Improvement of the Mind.* 8 Vols. (London, 1808). Reviewed and copiously (pp. 299-315) summarized in *Edinburgh Review* 15 (1810):301. Unavailable in the original.
34. Ibid., p. 304.
35. Ibid., p. 308.
36. Ibid.
37. Ibid., p. 313.
38. West, *Letters*, 3:108-9.
39. Mary Gwladys Jones, *Hannah More* (Cambridge: At the University Press, 1952), p. 114.
40. More, *Strictures, Works of More*, 5:323.
41. Ibid., p. 334.
42. Rousseau, *Émile*, p. 254.
43. More, *Strictures, Works of More*, 5:329.
44. Hannah More, *Coelebs in Search of a Wife* (1809; reprinted in *Collected Works*, 2 vols., New York: Harper & Bros., 1839), 2:308.
45. Hopkins, *Hannah More and Her Circle*, p. 16.
46. Elizabeth Hamilton, *Letters on the Elementary Principles of Education*, 2 vols. (London: Samuel Bishop, 1803), 1:256.
47. Ibid., p. 23 n.
48. West, *Letters*, 2:390.
49. Wollstonecraft, *Thoughts on the Education of Daughters with Reflections on Female Conduct, in the More Important Duties of Life* (London: J. Johnson, 1787), p. 145.
50. Henry Noel Brailsford, *Shelley, Godwin, and Their Circle* (New York: H. Holt & Co., 1913), pp. 196-99.
51. Frances Broadhurst, "A Word in Favour of Female Schools: Addressed to Parents, Guardians, and the Public at Large," *Pamphleteer* 27 (1826): 453-73.
52. Wollstonecraft, *Education of Daughters*, p. 58.
53. Ibid., p. 48.
54. Ibid., p. 36.
55. Ibid., p. 101.
56. Hopkins, *Hannah More and Her Circle*, p. 156.
57. Elie Halévy, *A History of the English People in 1815* (London: Penguin, 1924), p. 381.
58. More, *Memoirs*, 1:389.
59. Hopkins, *Hannah More and Her Circle*, p. 166.
60. Ibid., p. 169.

61. West, *Letters*, 3:323.

62. More to the earl of Oxford, 1793, in *Memoirs*, 1:427.

63. More to Montagu, 1784, in ibid., p. 207.

64. Hopkins, *Hannah More and Her Circle*, p. 123.

65. More, *Strictures, Works of More*, 5:322.

66. West, *Letters*, 1: frontispiece, Prov. 31:30.

67. Ibid., 2:385.

68. More, *Moral Sketches, Works of More*, 4:18.

69. E. Hamilton, *Letters on Principles of Education*, 2:296-97.

70. More, *Moral Sketches, Works of More*, 4:370.

71. Hopkins, *Hannah More and Her Circle*, p. 232.

72. Ibid., p. 179.

73. More, *Strictures, Works of More*, 5:332.

74. C. Willett Cunnington, *Feminine Attitudes in the Nineteenth Century* (New York: Macmillan Co., 1936), p. 92.

75. Ibid.

76. Jones, *Hannah More*, p. 205.

77. Hopkins, *Hannah More and Her Circle*, p. 210.

78. John Langdon-Davies, *A Short History of Women* (New York: Viking Press, 1927), pp. 345-46.

3
Mothers and Children:
The Relegated Roles

*The hand that rocks the cradle is the hand
that rules the world.*
— William Ross Wallace

*Female authors are undoubtedly distinguished
by an elegant discrimination of what is beautiful or disgusting: their taste is correct; their
imagination lively; their language easy, free
and polished; but we cannot allow them
strength of mind, deep reasoning powers, nor,
in every instance, that firm solid judgment
found in the other sex.*
— *Critical Review* (August 1804)

Until the nineteenth century children were not considered to
be very important to society. In the late eighteenth and early
nineteenth centuries, English women, mothers and governesses
especially, played an exclusive role in their upbringing. Even
after Rousseau, in 1762, called attention to their needs,
children were either in school or in the nursery and hence quite
removed from adult society. A child, relates historian Phillippe
Aries, "had to be subjected to a special treatment, a sort of

78

quarantine, before he was allowed to join the adults."[1]

Since women, too, were unimportant in adult society, it was only logical that they should be assigned the role of caring for children. As male children reached adolescence, when they were beginning to become socially important, their education was taken over by men. Although a child's morals and character were nurtured primarily by his mother and governesses and through the early stories he read, which were generally written by women, his father and tutors usually took the credit if he turned out well. Even if he turned out poorly, recriminations usually fell on his father and older brothers, for character, or lack of it, was thought to be devloped by the stronger forces in society, that is, by men. To set the record straight, the hand that rocked the cradle and even produced some of the early-nineteenth-century literature, did not rule the male world.

Women's writing, like their influence on their sons, was almost always minimized, even when successful. Few lawmakers, merchants, scientists, or landowners were ever influenced by women writers. If women wanted an audience, they had to write for other women or for children. Sometimes they wrote only for themselves.

In the late eighteenth and early nineteenth centuries, as a result of the influence of Locke, Rousseau, and the rise of Evangelicalism, concern for the education of young children was rising. Because of their helplessness and vulnerability, as well as the growing significance of the middle-class family, children were beginning to receive more attention, especially from their mothers, than ever before in history. If women were to write at all, it could be claimed that nothing was more fitting than discoursing on the rearing of children, women's primary and natural role. Even if they were childless or unmarried, women authors had definite opinions on childraising. Women who wrote books *for* children — to instruct as well as to entertain — were quite explicit in pointing out differences in male and female roles.

When in 1792 Mary Wollstonecraft wrote *A Vindication of the Rights of Women*, which stresses equality for women, she was severely attacked by women as well as men, not only for her public views but also for her private life. The story is familiar. She lived first with Gilbert Imlay and bore him a child out of wedlock; then with William Godwin, whom she married only when she learned she was pregnant. In many places *Vindication* was banned; it was, in the view of many, social heresy. This response is in marked contrast to that which greeted her *Thoughts on the Education of Daughters* only five years earlier. This work, primarily devoted to the rearing of infants and young children, was widely acclaimed. Years after *Vindication* appeared and was condemned, people still read and praised *Thoughts*. In fact, it was pirated by a Dublin printer, who issued it in the same volume with a translation of Archbishop Fénelon's rather pious instructions to a governess and an address to mothers.

Mary Wollstonecraft, who had read both Rousseau and Locke on the subject of child-rearing, incorporated much of their thinking into her own writing. Woman's primary duty, they all believed, was to take care of her children. During the late eighteenth and early nineteenth centuries, the use of wet nurses was relatively common among many upper-middle and upper-class women. While the absence of birth-control devices condemned these women to constant childbearing, they could free themselves from child rearing somewhat by sending their infants to the farms of peasant women until they were weaned. Rousseau, in book 1 of *Émile* decries this practice. "Do these polished mothers," he asks, "who escaped from their children [in order to] indulge themselves gaily in the amusements of the town know the treatment which their innocent babes in their swathings are enduring in the country?"[2] As Rousseau implied, many of the peasant women performed their wet-nurse services only for the money it brought them and, either from ignorance or disinterest, often neglected or even abused their infant charges.

Though Mary Wollstonecraft opposed many of Rousseau's nonegalitarian views on women, particularly his claims that

Mary Wollstonecraft
COURTESY OF THE NATIONAL PORTRAIT GALLERY, LONDON.

women were created to charm and please men and to live in subjection, she embraced his idea that mothers should take full responsibility for the weaning and upbringing of their off-spring. She felt that breast feeding develops in the child a "sturdy constitution," and more importantly, a tenderness between mother and child. (The role of the father toward the infant is not discussed by either writer. One can only conjecture, then, that child care was considered strictly a woman's job.)

Mary Wollstonecraft, however, also advised mothers on how to develop their children's minds. She urged them not to use baby talk with boys *or* girls, for, she says, it retards the development of their vocabularies. Moreover, she added, as the infant grows the mother should encourage it to think by making comparisons between things. Finally, mothers should teach children to understand information, not to memorize it.

Wollstonecraft's advice to mothers concerning their own behavior carried these ideas even further. She criticized women's superficial interest in learning, for how, she asked, can a mother raise intelligent children if she fails to take herself seriously? Wollstonecraft also discussed the role of the mother in caring for her children in *Vindication*, published five years after *Thoughts on the Education of Daughters*. "Unless the understanding of women be enlarged," she writes, "and her character rendered more firm, by being allowed to govern her own conduct, she will never have sufficient sense or command of temper to manage her children properly." According to her, education for women was crucial to their lives.

Although society downgraded women's role in inculcating character in their offspring once the children were older, all four of the women writers whose works on the rearing of children are considered here—Mary Wollstonecraft, Ann Taylor, Elizabeth Hamilton, and Anna L. Barbauld—were explicit in their views on the development of morals and self-discipline.

In *Thoughts on the Education of Daughters*, in a chapter on "Moral Discipline," Mary Wollstonecraft is both sensible and conservative. In it she advocates teaching the importance of order, honesty, submission to superiors (that is, parents and teachers), and proper management of inferiors (servants). She is also concerned with developing creativity in children, for she encourages mothers to nurture in their offspring a taste for music and painting, as well as for the beauties of nature. Mary Wollstonecraft believed that children should be encouraged to write stories expressing their sentiments and interests for their own entertainment. Despite the title of her book, however, she does not distinguish between the sexes. Her sensible advice to mothers is intended for both daughters and sons.

Reading *Thoughts on the Education of Daughters* must have been an encouraging experience. Although Mary Wollstonecraft was conservative in urging women to rear their own children, she was progressive in her view that mothers should be as fully educated as fathers and, therefore, that they be equal as human beings. Yet she was well aware that father and mother, as well as husband and wife, were not equal in the early nineteenth century. "Nothing," she says, "calls forth the faculties so much as the being obliged to struggle with the world; and this is not a woman's province in a married state." But such statements are rare in a book that concentrates on the cultivation of understanding, compassion, good sense, and moral discipline.

If Mary Wollstonecraft's views on equal treatment of the sexes are understated in *Thoughts on the Education of Daughters*, references to sexual equality are almost nonexistent in the works of Ann Taylor, Elizabeth Hamilton, and Anna L. Barbauld.

In *Practical Hints*, by Ann Taylor, one section on "Education" is devoted to advice on methods of raising children. Neither her position that women should remain in the home nor her advice on child rearing in general is original. Like Rousseau, who advocated more lenient treatment of children, Taylor believed that a child ought to be disciplined, but never by physical punishment or in public. Rather, parents could "endeavour to correct what is amiss, [rather] than to depreciate . . .[their children] in the esteem of others, and thus weaken one of the motives to honourable conduct."

In agreement with both her predecessor Rousseau, and her contemporary Wollstonecraft, Taylor acknowledges middle-class woman's domestic role, and, warning her readers that "servants. . .are, in general, too ignorant to be trusted much alone with children," urges mothers to remain at home. Most middle- and upper-class women did not, of course, work, but they did engage in other diversions, such as social and religious functions outside the home. "Mothers. . .in attending the public services of religion many times during the week," Taylor asserts, "are obliged to neglect those important duties which, as mothers, Providence has committed to their hands."

Elizabeth Hamilton's attitude toward bringing up children, as expressed in *Letters on the Elementary Principles of Education*, is more original than Ann Taylor's, but is naive as compared to Mary Wollstonecraft's. She presents some very sensible ideas—ideas that hardly differ from those of contemporary child psychologists—but she fails to explain how they can be implemented. She is, first of all, against overindulging children. "Where success is certain," she explains, "hope can have no existence; nor can joy be produced by that which is considered as a right." A child should have to work, to strive, in order to achieve recognition. The greater the effort, the more significant the results. Boys were taught to expect success, but girls were discouraged from competing with their brothers. "Let hope and joy be excluded from the human mind," she adds, "and where is happiness?" Hamilton lacked the foresight to realize, in the early nineteenth century, that a girl's hopes for eduction, for a profession, even for mere equality, were often, as she grew up, shattered.

She also thought that children should be encouraged to make intelligent choices at all times. The example she gives is common enough—a child who is noisily playing in the living room while his or her parents entertain should be asked to decide whether he or she wishes to remain and be quiet or go to his or her room to make noise. She never alludes to the fact, however, that females, even upper-class females, were not permitted to choose to study Greek instead of French, or to attend an academic school, to have a male tutor, or to enter a profession.

But Hamilton does comment on children's being forced into sexually defined roles early in life. She disagrees with Rousseau's claim that "there are special tastes that distinguish each sex." The example that Rousseau gives is that "boys like movement and noise — drums, tops, and hobby-horses; girls prefer decorations that please the eye — looking glasses, jewellery, baby clothes, and particularly, dolls. . .[which] are . . .[their] favourite amusement. . .a taste clearly based on their life work." Elizabeth Hamilton argues that, on the contrary, if a little girl is permitted "to follow the bent of her own inclination," often she prefers "beating the drum, or whipping the top with her brother, to dressing and undressing the finest doll in her possession." She attributes feminine interest in dolls and clothes to what we today call associative learning: for example, a little girl is usually praised for her finery so that when she grows up she devotes most of her effort to her physical appearance.

Despite Hamilton's writings, however, parents accepted, and hence perpetuated in their children the traditional masculine and feminine roles. Women textbook writers also amplified this sexism, as the example of Anna L. Barbauld, the former Anna Letitia Aikin (1743-1825), demonstrates. Barbauld's father, Dr. Aikin, was an assistant master at a small school, and her husband ran a boys' school. She not only kept the books and handled all financial matters, but also wrote lectures on geography and history and taught a class of younger boys.

Most women writers were concerned with the education of girls, superficial though it was, but Barbauld's essays on education dealt with the education of boys. Unlike Wollstonecraft, Taylor, and Hamilton, Barbauld minimized the role that parents play in the education of their children. Rather, she

favored "child masters and tutors [engaged] at large salaries."
When she does refer to the parental education of children, it is
the father who, in her system, does the educating. He instills
character in his son. Addressing fathers, she writes: "Your example will educate [your son]; your conversation with your
friends [not women's chit-chat], the business he sees you tran-
sact, the likings and dislikings you express, these will educate
him; . . .above all, your rank and situation in life, your house,
your table, your pleasure grounds, your hounds and your
stables will educate him."[3] Thus Barbauld seems to leave formal education to the male tutor and character formation to the
father. If woman plays any part at all, it receives no mention in
Barbauld's essay.

Illustrative of the ironies of the feminine attitude and similar
to the case of Hannah More, a woman writer who divorces
herself from her sex, is Barbauld's belief that women ought to
be "excused from all professional knowledge" — that is, "all
that is necessary to fit a man for a peculiar profession or
business." "Languages," adds Barbauld, "are on some ac-
counts particularly adapted to female study, as they may be
learned at home without experiments or apparatus, and
without interfering with the habits of domestic life. But the
learned languages, the Greek especially, require a good deal
more time than a young woman can conveniently spare."[4] As
for Latin, Barbauld advises it, except that knowledge of Latin
"will not in the present state of things excite either a smile or a
stare in fashionable company."[5] If women did not enter professions, if they were prohibited from male recreation, and if their
education was so watered down, it seems inevitable that they
would have *more time* in which to study languages. Furthermore, was not so-called fashionable company composed of
learned *men* who had studied Greek and Latin? "A woman is
not expected to understand the mysteries of politics," further
claims Barbauld, "because she is not called to govern; she is
not required to know anatomy, because she is not to perform
surgical operations." Yet Barbauld herself received a broad
education, which helped her to "govern" her husband's school

and write children's textbooks. For her pupils and her nephew she wrote *Early Lessons for Children* and *Hymns in Prose*, works that, according to J. W. Croker in *Quarterly Review*,

Anna L. Barbauld
COURTESY OF THE COURTAULD INSTITUTE OF ART, UNIVERSITY OF LONDON

"display not much of either taste or talents but are somewhat better than harmless." Clearly, women, even women writers, were taken seriously neither by themselves nor by men.

Women writers were, however, taken more seriously by children, for children's books were very popular. Around the turn of the nineteenth century, books for children had been uncommon. Among the women writers, only Hannah More opposed such works. "The too great profusion of them protracts the imbecility of childhood," she asserted. "They arrest the understanding instead of advancing it." Dr. Johnson, however, approved of stories designed for children. Indeed, he had very specific ideas about the kinds that children like to hear. "Babies do not like to hear stories of babies like themselves," he claimed. "They require to have their imaginations raised by tales of giants, and fairies, and enchantments."

Maria Edgeworth and her father, who jointly published *The Parent's Assistant; or, Stories for Children*, a book of moralistic children's stories, disagreed. "Children enjoy fairy tales but they soon perceive that fairies and giants are not to be met with in the world. Why not give them useful knowledge?" But while fairies and giants did not exist in the real world, discrimination against women did, and, ironically, women writers of children's pieces helped perpetuate their subordinate role.

Despite Hannah More's contrary opinion, children's books had a significant impact on character and morals, especially in defining the sexually connected roles that children would later have to assume as adults — roles that according to today's views are limited. Moreover, children's stories were usually well reviewed, albeit condescendingly, the consensus being that women excelled in this field. In the *Monthly Mirror* of December 1800, for example, the reviewer of a children's story entitled *The Asiatic Princess* by a little-known writer named Mrs. Pilkington, states that "Mrs. Pilkington has contributed so largely to the stock of harmless and innocent amusement."

Some early books for children combined both lessons and stories. Inspired by Anna L. Barbauld's *Early Lessons*, Sarah Trimmer (1741-1810) created *An Easy Introduction to the Knowledge of Nature*, later reprinted under the title *Easy Lessons; or, Leading Strings to Knowledge in Three Parts: The*

Sarah Trimmer
COURTESY OF THE NATIONAL PORTRAIT GALLERY, LONDON

First and Third Parts by a Lady for her Own Children: The Second Part Arranged by the Late Mrs. Trimmer. Part 2, Trimmer's contribution, is about a three-year-old boy and his six-year-old sister whose mother gives them a book containing thirteen broadly related stories. This is a frame story. The mother and her two children respond to, and comment on, the tales the mother relates.

Two of these stories illustrate how male and female roles, often inadvertently, were instilled in children. In "The Two Peacocks," the more attractive bird has a wretched personality, demonstrating that physical beauty is only skin deep. The little boy in the frame tells his mother that he "will not be cross like the proud peacock." His sister also gets the point — for she vows "never [to] be proud or vain." If she wants "the love of good people," she explains, she must be "humble and meek, and kind and good-natured." The implication is that men, clearly the more forceful sex, should not abuse their superiority by being "cross," bad-tempered, and tyrannical. And women must practice humility and meekness, for they were more often praised for their goodness and piety than for their beauty. Hence, woman's subordination and passivity were reinforced very early.

A second tale, "The Owl in the Hollow Tree," is especially poignant, considering how many early-nineteenth-century women died in childbirth, leaving children with a series of stepmothers, women who often took an interest only in their own natural chidren and neglected those of their predecessors. The story's central interest is in an uncaring mother owl, who is especially cruel to her sickliest child, Tiny. But Tiny resolves to remain "obedient" to her mother and "by patience and submission. . .[to] endeavour to please her." One day the mother returns home badly injured, after being almost totally crushed in a trap. All her children ignore her — except Tiny, who nurses her. She therefore come to favor Tiny, who in turn finds "that good-humour and gentleness will make even the most ill-tempered creature kind and obliging." It is no coincidence that the kind, gentle owl that endures its mother's "ill-tempered" behavior with "patience and submission" is a *female* owl. A young child who might have to live with a cruel stepmother might eventually become a married woman who must endure her husband's "ill-temper." Therefore, girls were advised, early in life, to be forebearing of such behavior.

Following the stories, the mother in the frame explains to the children what their respective educations will be. Characteristically, the girl's is different from the boy's. Mary will learn only French, whereas William will master French, Latin, Greek, and many other languages. Barbauld ascribes this dual standard to "custom." In her writings she explains that "custom has made the one [French] as much expected from an accomplished woman, as the other (Latin or Greek] from a man who has had a liberal education." Since an upper-class woman functioned primarily in the drawing room, she merely had to be charming. But it was assumed that a successful upper-class man, who traveled, conducted business, and participated in politics, had to be broadly educated.

Maria Edgeworth, whose name, according to one critic, became "a household word," also subscribed to the dual standard for men and women. After Maria's mother died, her father, Richard Edgeworth, had three wives and each bore him children. Richard Edgeworth, who was very interested in education, had been influenced by the writings of Rousseau. He encouraged Maria to write stories for her younger brothers and sisters. On the basis of their responses and criticism, Maria would edit and revise them. In 1796 she and her father published ten of these narratives under the title *The Parent's Assistant: or, Stories for Children*. This title is important in terms of educating children, but one cannot help realizing the implication, especially after reading Anna L. Barbauld's advice to fathers, that the mother, who would most probably read the stories to her children, was merely the father's "assistant." A second edition of the work containing additional stories followed later that year, and in 1800 a third edition, in six volumes and comprising more than twenty stories, appeared. The tales in *The Parent's Assistant* were, claimed Edgeworth, "emphatically stories with a purpose; virtue is always rewarded and craft and roguery are sure to defeat their own ends." In addition, Edgeworth's stories for children were the first of their kind to have real plots, suspense, surprises, and even excitement. But, most significantly, for all their efforts to instill moral honesty, the stories clearly depict conventional sexist roles. While Maria Edgeworth admits in the preface to *The Parent's Assistant* that "the education of different ranks should, in some respects, be different" because "they have few ideas, few habits in common," she fails to say that the education of the sexes was also different, even though girls and boys could have "ideas and habits in common." Furthermore, even though she acknowledges that "truth and humanity should be enforced with equal care and energy upon the minds of young people of every station," the role differences between the sexes are amplified in her stories. The aggressive roles are nearly always assumed by males, the passive, by females, as three of the narratives reveal.

In "The Orphans," five good little orphans discover a batch of gold coins buried under the chimney of an old castle where they seek shelter. They later visit two young, kindly, upper-middle-class, urban ladies to learn if the coins are authentic. To prevent readers of the story from having any doubt about class superiority, the narrator explains that "it is not only by their superior riches, but it is yet more by their superior knowledge, that persons in the higher rank of life [the ladies] may assist those in a lower condition."

A rich but dishonest man commandeers the "poor children's" coins, sells them, and subsequently accuses the children of having stolen the coins. While most people believe him, the children continue to work diligently and to be polite and respectful. With the aid of the ladies, the children are ultimately exonerated and, "as a reward for their honesty," are given a little slatted house. Hannah More would probably have

Maria Edgeworth
COURTESY OF THE NATIONAL PORTRAIT GALLERY, LONDON

objected to the outcome, for she believed that the poor should expect, and receive, no reward.

The role implications in the story are obvious. The eldest orphan, a girl, takes care of her younger brothers and sisters—assuming a mother's role. While the upper-middle-class ladies are charitable and virtuous, the dominant roles in the story are assumed by men. An aggressive man is villainous and steals the children's coins, and a rich and generous man rewards them by giving them a house to live in.

Another of Maria Edgeworth's tales, "Lazy Lawrence," contrasts two young men: a good, simple, industrious lad, Jem, who works first as a gardener's assistant and then as a mat-maker, and Lawrence, the son of a drunkard, who is a lazy good-for-nothing. One of the story's morals is that idleness breeds crime.

Honest Jem works hard and earns enough money to keep his mother's horse, which she was planning to sell in order to buy food for her family (a woman needs a man, husband or son, so that she and her family can survive). After Lazy Lawrence and his wicked friend steal the money that Jem has saved, the narrator provides a rather lengthy and pious description of Lawrence's psychological reaction. "All night he was starting from frightful dreams. . .and was tormented by that most dreadful of all kinds of fear, that fear which is the constant companion of an evil conscience."

Eventually, Lawrence and his friend are apprehended and imprisoned—and for all her moralism, Maria Edgeworth fails to perceive the horror of jailing a child. Evidently, she will go to almost any extreme to frighten children into being honest. Jem forgives Lawrence, visits him in jail, and brings him small gifts. After all, we are told, "Jem could afford to be *generous* because he was industrious." Lawrence's heart is so touched by Jem's kindness and moral example that he resolves to go to work when his confinement ends, and he does. Thus two extremes of character are portrayed—weakness, actually crim-

inality, versus dedication and moral fortitude and, characteristically, the characters who embody these traits are male.
Females were too shallow even to be portrayed as criminals. In
adult novels, women become criminals and outcasts only
because they weakly succumb to immoral men.

The most complex of Edgeworth's stories is "Simple Susan,"
and the title proves ironic. This story does not, as one might expect, exclusively praise the virtues of the diligent poor. Rather,
it also mocks the newly monied members of the middle class
who lack both the breeding and style of the upper class and the
honesty and simplicity of the working class. Maria Edgeworth
uses female characters to illustrate the contrast between the
two classes, a contrast that is basically superficial. A greedy
lawyer's daughter, Barbara, tries to put on airs, but she is really self-serving and a conniver. Her character faults are consistently shown up by the behavior of Simple Susan, who is
poor, pretty and kind. Barbara's horrid brother's brutality is
explained by the fact that "his father had neglected to correct
his temper when he was a child, and, as he grew up, it became
insufferable." In the end, Barbara, her father, and her brother
are forced to leave town, and Susan and her family remain and
live happily. Thus when girls are nasty, they do not commit
criminals acts, as did Lazy Lawrence. Instead they are selfish,
jealous, and not above resorting to petty trickery. When they
are good, they do not, like Jem, make great sacrifices; they are
merely sweet and kind.

Each story conveys a valuable moral, encouraging the young
reader to say to himself: "I'll be sure not to end up like
Lawrence or Barbara," or whomever. But the younger reader
would also identify and associate certain character traits as
belonging to one sex or the other. In forming the characters of
youngsters, the women writers of children's stories obviously
played a significant role. And their role in influencing male-
female behavior and expectations was equally important.

NOTES

1. Phillippe Aries, *Centuries of Childhood: A Social History of Family Life* (New York: Vintage, 1962), p. 412.
2. Jean Jacques Rousseau, *Émile; or, Education*, trans. Barbara Foxley (1762: reprint ed., New York: E. P. Dutton & Co., 1911), p. 72.
3. Anna Laetitia Barbauld, *A Selection from the Poems and Prose Writings of Mrs. Anna Laetitia Barbauld*, ed. Grace A. Ellis (Boston: Roberts Bros., 1874), p. 246.
4. Ibid., p. 280.
5. Ibid.

4
Self-Expression
and Catharsis:
The Role of the Memoir

*I had so much rather live than write; writing is
only a substitute for living. . .I think one's feelings waste themselves in words; they ought all
to be distilled into actions which bring results.*
— Florence Nightingale

While some women writers wrote to instruct women in education and religion and child-rearing, and others created a fictional but nonetheless moral world to entertain children, still
another group wrote diaries, journals, and letters, ostensibly
for their own edification. Many of the better-known women
writers of the period, such as Hannah More and Fanny
Burney, kept some sort of journal. These journals are very
revealing in terms of how early-nineteenth-century women saw
themselves and their place in society. In the case of Dorothy
Wordsworth and Hester Stanhope, personal journals and letters were their sole literary output. For Mary Martha Butt
Sherwood, who also wrote many exemplary novels — especially

for Sunday school girls and for children — journals constitute a good portion of her literary effort. Although these three women used the same literary form, the personal journal, their characters and ways of life differed markedly.

Nevertheless, each woman was forced to occupy a subordinate position in English society. Mary Martha Butt Sherwood, a member of the upper-middle class, channeled her energies into helping the poor, especially children, acceptably fulfilling the role of an early-nineteenth-century woman of her class. Dorothy Wordsworth, who was middle class, and of a more literary and introspective bent than Sherwood, devoted her life to her brother. Hester Stanhope, a member of the upper class, which had more tolerance for unconventional behavior, traveled about and finally settled in the Middle East, where she attempted, however unsuccessfully, to "rule" over her estate. Still, each woman wrote primarily about herself, thus enabling contemporary readers to gain a greater understanding of the dilemma of women in nineteenth-century society.

The Life of Mrs. [*Mary Martha Butt*] *Sherwood with Extracts from Mr. Sherwood's Journal during his Imprisonment in France and Residence in India,* edited by Sherwood's daughter, is a perspicuous journal of an upper-middle-class woman — sensitive, charitable, religious, a thoroughly supportive wife and a tender and loving mother. In short, Sherwood exemplified Hannah More's concept of feminine perfection. But unlike More, whose faith in God was revealed primarily in her writings, Sherwood's was demonstrated by her daily activities.

What was unusual for the time was her upbringing at the hands of enlightened parents. Like Hannah More and Anna L. Barbauld, her father, George Butt, ran a school, and some of his pupils lived in. Mary was also very close to her brother, Marten, as were Fanny Burney and Dorothy Wordsworth to their brothers. They read books together, and when Marten had difficulty learning Latin, it was suggested that Mary be taught with him. In fact, their mother began to study Latin so that she could tutor her children. This situation, however, of a mother and daughter's learning what was traditionally a man's language, was the exception rather than the rule. Still, the women would not have learned it if it had been solely for their own edification and not to help their son and brother.

A young boy, George Annesley, who was three or four years older than Mary, came to live with the Butts; Mary, her brother, Marten, and George formed a friendly threesome, and this probably contributed significantly to Mary's education. "Even before I was twelve," she wrote, "I was obliged to translate fifty lines of Virgil every morning."[1] During much of the day Mary had to wear an iron collar—to discipline her mind as well as her body—while she stood and recited her Latin and other lessons. Inspired by Fanny Burney's *Cecilia*, she tried her hand at writing a novel but never completed it. And her "poor plays," she added, "never went beyond. . .[her] father's parlour."[2]

As rigorous as Mary's education was for that time, she admitted that while her learning was going on "in quiet England, Henry [her cousin and husband-to-be] was brought up in a more trying school."[3]

Unable to put her classical education to use as a teacher—for women could instruct only very young children, not adolescent males—and being completely barred from other professions such as law and medicine, where a background in Greek and Latin would be valuable, Mary along with her sister, did charity work. During an unusually cold winter in 1801, the Butt sisters worked all day making clothes for the poor, and in the evenings distributed the clothes, as well as bread, butter, tea, and sugar, which they bought with their own money.

Mary, in a sense the prototypical nineteenth-century woman, married the man whom her parents selected for her. He was Henry Sherwood, an English officer and her cousin. Not long after they were married, he was sent to Calcutta. In order to accompany him, Mary Sherwood had to leave their child, an infant, with her sister in England, because her doctor advised against transporting the baby. Of course, her husband came first, but Sherwood eagerly devoted her efforts to helping others, especially children. On the ship leaving England she began to teach. Her first pupil, whom she taught to read, was the ten-year-old son of a soldier.

With her husband, she continued to live a large part of her life in India, despite such obstacles as communication barriers, an unfavorable climate, cultural differences, and, since there were frequent outbreaks of fighting, physical danger. Children continued to be her main interest. She herself bore six, of whom only two survived. Her profound compassion and keen humanity are evidenced in her description of the intense grief that she experienced on the death in infancy of her first son, Henry. She wrote that many people thought that her "grief for Henry was inordinate," and she did not dispute the point, for she explained: "I am not writing these memoirs to prove myself a faultless person."[4]

She also adopted children, established nurseries, and founded schools for orphans. The enrollment in her first school quickly increased from thirteen to about forty or fifty children. She took care of their medical and nutritional requirements as well as tending to their emotional needs. At one point she related the incident concerning a cruel woman who had been asked to take care of a motherless infant. The woman was actually starving the child but persuaded the father that the child was ill. Sherwood detected the truth, took the child, and nursed it back to health.

Still, in her schools she was very careful to observe the conventions of the British class system. She criticized schools for orphans that "class together all the destitute children of European soldiers, without any respect to the colour of the mother, or her character as wife or otherwise. . . . It was not right and an offence to propriety to class the daughters of

English women of good character with children which had been nurtured by Hindoo and Mussulman mothers of the lowest description."

Although she believed in the class system, her compassion never faltered. When she came upon a little white boy "riding" a little Indian boy, she reprimanded the white boy's mother, who retorted that the Indian was her son's "slave." Sherwood, however, "unhorsed" the white boy and ordered him never to "ride" the Indian child.

In addition, unlike many other supposedly more enlightened women of her time, Sherwood had great compassion for her own sex. She lamented an outrage that most people pretended did not even exist: the sexual double standard that permitted white soldiers to exploit Indian women. The men kept their native mistresses in huts near the barracks; the women served the men and were faithful to them, and the orphanage provided a refuge for their children. But, Sherwood pointed out, there was no provision for the mother when the man left. "She has lost caste by her union with the white man," she wrote, "and has no resource but, if she can, to form such another temporary union with another white man."

Yet even Sherwood had her blind spots. She criticized Eastern women who could not, she stated, "use the needle" and, she added, "very few are taught any other feminine accomplishment." She was, understandably, conditioned to seeing women perform certain roles, and she mistakenly believed that the lives of these women were significantly different from those of upper-class English women. She imagined nothing to be more "monotonous" than the lives of Eastern women, with the exception of those in servile labor. According to Sherwood, the middle- and upper-class Eastern women "sit on their cushions, behind their curtains, from day to day, from month to month, with no other occupation than that of having their hair dressed and their nails and eyelids stained and no other amusement than. . .gossip." Actually, the differences between

Indian women of high caste and British women of breeding were primarily cultural. In other respects, they had much in common.

While Sherwood directed her energies toward serving helpless children and attempting to alleviate some of the stress placed by the extant social order on helpless women, Dorothy Wordsworth remained a spinster and focused her energies on her brother William. Both women, however, continually rendered service to others, the only acceptable role for women in early-nineteenth-century England.

Even though Dorothy Wordsworth's *Journals* were never intended for publication and were not published during her lifetime, they reveal more vividly than most published works her acceptance, as a matter of course, of the normal subordinate role assigned to women, however gifted. Nonetheless, echoes of her observations and descriptions appear quite frequently in her brother's poetry. Margaret Oliphant, in her *Literary History of England*, describes their relationship: William Wordsworth, she writes, was "the spokesman to the world of two souls. It was not that Dorothy visibly or consciously aided or stimulated [him], but that she was a part of him, a second pair of eyes to see, a second and more delicate intuition to discern. She was part not only of his life but of his imagination. He saw by her, felt through her. . .her journals are Wordsworth in prose, just as his poems are Dorothy in verse."[5] This description of their relationship clearly supports the role of the female as being submissive, that of the male as being dominant. Dorothy had "delicate intuition," the ability to see and feel beauty, and to relate her thoughts to her brother, but it was William, although he acknowledged his indebtedness to his sister in "Tintern Abbey," for instance, who actually wrote the poetry, and therefore received the recognition.

Although Margaret Oliphant recognized the closeness between William and Dorothy, she failed to perceive that, in

Dorothy Wordsworth
(Present owner unknown.)
COURTESY OF THE NATIONAL PORTRAIT GALLERY, LONDON

some cases, Dorothy's vision antedated William's. It was Dorothy who planted seeds that at times grew to fruition in William's mind and art. From the following examples it is clear that Wordsworth used Dorothy's sensitive and moving observations and descriptions, recorded in her diary, in his poetry. One spring morning in 1800, for instance, a woman with a ragged two-year-old child came to the house begging, and Dorothy gave her a piece of bread. Later that day she saw the woman's husband with two sons. When the boys came to beg, Dorothy said that she had "served" their mother in the morning. The boys insisted that their mother was dead, but Dorothy gave them nothing. William, who was actually away from home at the time, later used the incident in his poem "Beggars," written in 1802:

> They dart across my path—but lo,
> Each ready with a plaintive whine.
> Said I, "not half an hour ago
> Your mother has had alms of mine."
>
> "That cannot be," one answered. . ."she
>   is dead:"—
> I looked reproof—they saw—but neither
>   hung his head.
>
> "She has been dead, Sir, many a day."—
> "Hush, boys! You're telling me a lie:
> It was your mother as I say!"
> And in the twinkling of an eye,
> "Come! Come!" cried one, and without
>   more ado,
> Off to some other play the joyous Vagrants
>   flew!
>
> (ll. 37-48)

William Wordsworth's poem "Alice Fell," also composed in 1802, indicates his further indebtedness to Dorothy. Alice Fell was a poor orphan girl whose cloak, caught in the wheel of a chaise, was torn to rags. A friend of the Wordsworth's left money with a local family to buy Alice a new cloak. Similarly, Dorothy's meeting with an old retired sailor, including a precise description of his clothes and demeanor, is used in Book 9 of *The Prelude*.

Dorothy's journals also indicate the deep love and affection that she shared with her brother. "We sate in deep silence at the window — I on a chair and William with his hand on my shoulder. We were deep in Silence and Love, a blessed hour." Or "riding in a shower on the outside of a coach," they "buttoned [them] selves up both together in the Guard's coat, and we liked the hills and the Rain the better for bringing us so close to one another — I never rode more snugly."[6]

One biographer of Dorothy Wordsworth, Margaret Willy, contends that "no higher tribute could have been paid to the intuitive sympathy and selfless love of one who, subordinating her literary gifts to her brother's genius, still remains a word-artist in her own right."[7] But Willy's comment is naive, for Dorothy's "selfless love" was not unusual for her time; most women, married or single, were subserviently devoted to the men in their lives. They had little other choice. While William Wordsworth's poetry has been universally acclaimed, few students ever learn about Dorothy's journals. Even so, such an evaluation could be made only in retrospect, since Dorothy's writings, which provide a vivid picture of the life and people of a typical village community at the beginning of the 1800s, were not made public until years after her death. As for Dorothy Wordsworth the "word-artist," she was also Dorothy Wordsworth the nineteenth-century woman, who had to play a socially prescribed role. Throughout her diary, for example, she mentions having to do such chores as ironing, baking, cooking, and sewing. She even whitewashed the walls and ceiling of the Wordsworth cottage. Today, these seem like menial and arduous tasks for so brilliant and sensitive a woman as Dorothy undoubtedly was, but it must be remembered that she tacitly accepted these chores—in short, she was a victim of society.

Like Hannah More, Maria Edgeworth, and other so-called intellectual women, Dorothy was often ailing. She was plagued by headaches—nearly every third entry in Dorothy's diary mentions some illness—which were thought by experts to be caused by overtaxing the female brain. The real cause lay largely in reading "fine print, [by] flickering candlelight. . . [with] faulty eye-glasses."[8] Mary Hopkins, one of Hannah More's biographers, suggests that they may have been psychosomatically caused as well—for, in writing at all, these women were defying society.

Hester Stanhope also attempted to defy woman's passive role. Perhaps more than almost any other nineteenth-century woman, Stanhope attempted to rebel against the female position. From her frequent disguises in male attire and her pipe smoking, to her leaving England to live in Eastern Europe, where she "ruled" over her estate and captivated many visitors, Stanhope sought always to exercise her independence.

As a child she had received an upper-class upbringing. Her mother died when she was four. Her father and stepmother were too absorbed in their social lives and travels to pay much attention to her or to their other children. In fact, her sister, Lucy, used to say that if she were to meet her stepmother in the street, she would not recognize her.

When she was twenty-seven, Stanhope moved in with her uncle, William Pitt. The apple of his eye and the recipient of his generosity, Hester was able to indulge all her fancies. When Pitt became prime minister of England for the second time, Lady Hester found herself in a position of great social importance. Like her contemporary Hannah More, who also mixed well in male society, she looked down on other women. Stanhope also resembled Hannah More in her ethereal quality. For instance, William Pitt used to say to her, she related: "Hester, what sort of being are you? We shall see, some day, wings spring out of your shoulders; for there are moments when you hardly seem to walk the earth?"[9]

Describing the dinners at her uncle's home, she wrote: "Military and naval characters are constantly *welcome* here; women are not, I *suppose*, because they do not form any part of our society."[10] Stanhope prided herself on her independence and on her interest in politics and current affairs, as opposed to being involved with petty gossip and dress, the predominant interests of most upper-class women. But a further comment indicates that she may also have viewed other attractive women as a threat, for she explains: "You may guess, then, what a pretty fuss they make with me?"[11]

She had many suitors, but perhaps the real reason that Hester Stanhope never married — in an age when marriage was the *only* acceptable life for a woman — is revealed in the following conversation. A friend of William Pitt's remarked of Hester's single state: "I suppose she waits till she can get a man as clever as herself." "Then," answered Pitt, "she will never marry at all." Not only was Hester well informed, but she was also outspoken and competitive, and most men, even sophisticated men, still preferred quiet, passive, non-competitive women.

"There is not a man in my kingdom who is a better politician than Lady Hester," said King George III, adding "there is not a woman who adorns her sex more than she does." But this was empty flattery. Although many other great and powerful men in England recognized Stanhope's intelligence, she was never given a position of power.

Qualified to lead but unable to do so, at least in England, Stanhope left the country several years after Pitt's death, when she was thirty-five. She set out in 1810 with a large retinue of servants, a lover several years her junior, and her physician, Dr. Meryon, who would later compile her *Memoirs*. After a long and arduous journey, all finally settled in Syria in a huge abandoned monastery.

Stanhope built stables, cottages, offices, and entire villages, and employed many local servants, over all of whom she attempted to rule. Despite one friend's description of her as "sensible, well-informed, and extremely shrewd with. . .extraordinary powers of conversation," she was also generous and gullible.[12] Perhaps her three most outstanding traits, as revealed in her letters and diaries (mostly recorded by her niece, in the third person), were her compassion, her eccentricity, and her propensity to lead. The first two characteristics, however, appear to have eclipsed the third. "A surer friend, a more frank and generous enemy, never trod the earth," said Dr. Meryon. " 'Show me where the poor and needy are,' she would say, and 'let the rich shift for themselves.' " In her later years, when she had only £20, Dr. Meryon recounted, Stanhope ordered him to give some of it to a leper, a distressed shopkeeper, and a few other pensioners. In addition, she daily sent fruit and other foods, plus clothing, to Dr. Meryon's family. She was consistently humanitarian and liberal. For example, when two unmarried slaves produced a child out of wedlock, "she sent for the offenders, insisted on their instant marriage and set them free."

Not all of her actions were as sensible. According to Armstrong in his biography of Hester Stanhope, "when a [male] fortune-teller told her 'she would one day go to Jerusalem and lead back the chosen people,' she half-heartedly believed it" and supported the man—and another who made the same prediction—for years. She was also quite superstitious, and refused to do business on certain days that she considered unlucky.

Like most male leaders in those days, Stanhope believed in herself. She had, her niece related, "an unbounded confidence in her own powers" and "she. . .displayed a rare aptitude for government in the management of the half-civilized, credulous and emotional people with whom she had to deal." Only in a country outside of England, however, could Stanhope exercise what male contemporaries—and women—might have called "masculine" qualities and talents. Essentially, she spent much of her life, attested her physician, "in giving orders, scoldings, writing letters and holding those interminable conversations

Hester Stanhope
COURTESY OF THE COURTAULD INSTITUTE OF ART, UNIVERSITY OF LONDON

which filled so large a portion of her time, and seemed so necessary to her."

Although Stanhope, at least in part because she was a

woman, had been unable to fulfill her potential for leadership in England, she also, like Hannah More and Anna L. Barbauld, discriminated against her own sex. Even Dr. Meryon spoke of "the extraordinary hatred that Lady Hester Stanhope bore to her own sex," although he claimed not to have known why. Perhaps it was easier to subscribe to society's attitudes than to fight them, or perhaps these more intelligent and creative women found it easier to identify with men. At any rate, Dr. Meryon explained that, during Stanhope's travels, whenever she was visited by men, their wives were never included. Moreover, he added that she admitted to him her general dislike for women, saying that of all the hundreds of females she had met, there were very few of whom she could speak well. The narrowness of women's minds, the triviality of their lives, which are probably what Hester objected to, were, of course, the result of society's attitudes and institutions.

Commenting on women's desire to spend their evenings with their husbands, Stanhope claimed that "all sensible men that I have ever heard of take their meals with their wives, and then retire to their own room to read, write, or do what they have to do, or what best pleases them." She listed the following examples: "If a man is a fox-hunter, he goes and talks with his huntsmen or the grooms. . .and if he is a tradesman, he goes into his shop; if a doctor, to his patients; but nobody is such a fool as to moider away his time in the slip-slop conversation of a pack of women." Obviously Stanhope was contemptuous because women were not articulate about topics that were considered important, not only to their husbands, but to Stanhope herself. She also condemned the poor care that English mothers gave their children. "They bring [the child] into the world, and know no more the duties of a mother—no, not so well as the sheep and the asses."

There was one woman of whom Stanhope spoke affectionately in her letters and diary and to Dr. Meryon—the novelist Lady Charlotte Bury. She even expressed a desire to have Lady Charlotte visit her in Syria, but abandoned the idea because of lack of funds. But once again Stanhope expressed a male attitude toward women. Although she read and enjoyed Charlotte Bury's works, she praised only the author's physical attributes. "What a beautiful woman she was," Hester exclaimed, referring to the time she saw Lady Charlotte at the opera, and she adds: "She walked so. . .graceful[ly]."

Despite her aversion to the female sex, Hester Stanhope was vain about her physical appearance even in her old age. When a German prince wrote a long philosophical letter begging to see her in order to converse, she answered his letter as follows: "Is it your object, in coming here, to laugh at a poor creature, reduced by sickness to skin and bone, who has lost half her sight and all her teeth?"

For a woman who had once enjoyed financial independence, audiences with great and learned men, the opportunity to rule over many servants, male and female—such "pomp and power," as Dr. Meryon put it—Hester's last years were pathetic. In fact, she was almost destitute. Many of her foreign servants, people to whom she had been kind, later mistreated her. When she was bedridden because of a severe illness, "all her attendants fled and left her to perish" and, as she lay helpless, "robbers came and carried away her property." After months of reading Hester's memoirs, her niece praised Hester's "striking and original character," but lamented Hester's sad fate: "She who had helped and befriended so many found no one to stand by her in her sorest need, and died bereft of [nearly] all human aid and consolation."

Even on her deathbed, Dr. Meryon explained, Hester maintained a "terrific vitality." She lay there "with her pipe in her mouth talking on politics, philosophy, morality, religion, or on any other theme, with her accustomed eloquence." Perhaps, then, what was most pathetic about Hester's later life was not her ill health or her shabby surroundings or her loss of wealth, but rather the fact that she could not have been a man, for only then could she perhaps have fulfilled her potential.

One must remember, however, that although Hester led a generally interesting life, because she was a woman who defied convention she was socially ostracized. What is more, she remained a spinster, and the ill-treatment of spinsters—even spinsters of the upper class—was, as Ann Taylor said, "a species of cruelty in which both sexes [were] apt to indulge." Similarly, in the *Critical Review*, a male writer stated that "an old maid has not. . .a heart open to social affections."[3] This was definitely untrue of Hester Stanhope.

Clearly, with the exception of a few women of the upper class like Lady Hester Stanhope, most early-nineteenth-century women followed the dictates of society, and, in case they had any doubts about the behavior expected of them, books by women writers told them and their children how to behave, even though some of these writers themselves behaved differently. The practice of women writers in defining women's proper role is, as will become evident, particularly characteristic of the most popular and influential genre of all—the novel.

NOTES

1. Mary Martha Butt Sherwood, *The Life of Mrs. Sherwood (chiefly autobiographical) with Extracts from Mr. Sherwood's Journal during his Imprisonment in France and Residence in India*, ed. her daughter, Sophia Kelly (London: Darton, 1854), p. 54.
2. Ibid., p. 79.
3. Mary Martha Butt Sherwood, *The Life of Mrs. Sherwood Written by Herself with Extracts from Mr. Sherwood's Journal during His Imprisonment in France and Residence in India*, abridged from London edition (Boston: American Tract Society, 1864), p. 139.
4. Sherwood, *Life of Mrs. Sherwood* (chiefly autobiographical), p. 329.
5. Margaret Oliphant, *Literary History of England*, 3 vols. (London: Macmillan & Co., 1894), 1:223.
6. Margaret Willy, *Three Women Diarists* (London: Longmans, 1964), p. 24.
7. Ibid., pp. 30-31.
8. Mary Alden Hopkins, *Hannah More and Her Circle* (New York: Longmans, Green & Co., 1947), p. 197.

9. Lady Hester Stanhope, *Memoirs of the Lady Hester Stanhope as Related by Herself in Conversations with Her Physician, Charles Lewis Meryon,* 3 vols. (London: H. Colburn, 1845), 2:20.

10. Martin Armstrong, *Lady Hester Stanhope* (New York: Viking Press, 1928), p. 23.

11. Ibid.

12. Lady Hester Stanhope, *The Life and Letters of Lady Hester Stanhope by Her Niece, the Duchess of Cleveland* (London: Clowes, 1897), p. 338.

13. *Critical Review* 6 (July 1814): 165.

5
Wives and Servants: Proper Conduct for One's Proper Place

The Novel is a picture of real life and manners and of the times in which it is written.[1]
—Clara Reeve

The rich should be superior in knowledge to the poor in order to maintain the society, and men to women.[2]
—Review of *The Letters of Mrs. Elizabeth Montagu*

The ideal woman—pious, pure, submissive, and domestic—described by early-nineteenth-century women writers in their nonfiction works was also lauded in the novel. As Vineta Colby explains in *Yesterday's Woman: Domestic Realism in the English Novel*, "The relationship between educational theory and fictional practice was very close in the early nineteenth century." She further observes that as "education came to be regarded as child-centered and therefore a function of the home, the novel became. . .female dominated."[3]

During the latter part of the eighteenth century and throughout the nineteenth century the novel flourished. A master's thesis entitled "The Lesser Novel: 1770-1800," written by a Miss Husbands for the University of London, lists no less than thirteen hundred novels. It is hard to determine exactly how many of the thirteen hundred were by women. Out of a handful of famous major novelists during the last quarter of the eighteenth century and the first quarter of the nineteenth century, the *Cambridge Bibliography of English Literature* lists only three female authors: Fanny Burney, Jane Austen, and Maria Edgeworth. The list of *minor* novelists from 1800 to 1835 includes thirty-six women and thirty-eight men. The male novelists of this period generally wrote fewer works than the females, their narratives were mainly adventure stories, and their protagonists were men.

According to Wilbur Cross in *The Development of the English Novel*, Richardson's contributions to the novel were "the sentimental young lady, the villain, and the abduction." Fielding was responsible for "the intrigue, the adventure, the singular character, and the kindhearted gentlemen."[4] Predictably, women's contribution was the faithful portrayal of women in society.

Although women writers faithfully recorded, as well as reinforced, society's view of woman and her role, little or no contemporary history appears in these novels—no mention of the French Revolution, the Wars against Napoleon, industrialization (and the part men and women played in it), or parliamentary issues. Fanny Burney offers the following explanation of the nonpolitical nature of these works. "I have felt, indeed, no disposition—I ought rather, perhaps, to say talent—for venturing upon the stormy sea of politics, whose waves, forever either receding or encroaching, with difficulty can be stemmed and never can be trusted."[5] Obviously, women, feeling that they could not "be trusted" to write about what was to them unknown, concentrated on a subject they knew best—women's lives. But even self-knowledge has its drawbacks, as Ernest

Baker, the literary historian, realized. Baker explains that, although the novels of the period may be "interesting or lively," the characterizations are strictly "two-dimensional."[6] But so, at the time, were women's lives, and of this limitation many women authors were faithful scribes.

One might indeed argue that middle- and upper-class women began to write simply because of the "two-dimensionality" of their lives. To these women, with abundant leisure time and few outlets for their energies, novel writing was instructive, or creative, or both. They could fulfill their moral purpose — the extolling of the feminine virtues, as established by society, and the warning of women of the dreadful consequences of promiscuity, vanity, selfishness, and aggression. Taking a more creative turn, some of the female novelists also filled their pages with vivid and moving descriptions of nature, with the histories of other nations (derived from their own readings), with the social patterns of various classes, and (possibly for pure escapism) with supernatural occurrences.

Another less altruistic motive for writing was money. One woman writer, for example, who wrote to support her eight fatherless children, assured her readers that "inclination had no share in her feeble attempts to entertain the Public."[7] Another testified that her latest literary work was "written by the bedside of a sick husband, who [had] no other support than what. . .[her] writing will produce."[8] Few novels appeared in less than two volumes; many comprised six or seven. In her lifetime Maria Edgeworth published forty-seven volumes. Authors were paid according to length; consequently, economy was rarely in evidence.

Despite such circumstances, which led to the emergence of female as well as male hacks, there appeared a number of very competent women novelists, of whom Fanny Burney and Maria Edgeworth were but two. Neither narrative content nor prolific output, however, convinced men that women writers were either as serious or as able as their male counterparts.

A typical comment on women writers from a male reviewer appeared in the October 1813 edition of the *Quarterly Review*. "With the single exception of Lady Mary Wortley Montagu [who wrote during the eighteenth century], no English woman before the present reign [has] produced a book that is still read, and still popular."[9] This critical bias is further suggested in a review of Mary Russell Mitford's narrative poems. "When she attempts to describe the higher passions. . .she fails from want of strength for the flight. But in the description of natural scenery, or the delineation of humbler and calmer feelings, she is more successful."[10]

The *Critical Review* similarly denigrated women writers: "Female authors are undoubtedly distinguished by an elegant discrimination of what is beautiful or disgusting: their taste is correct; their imagination lively; their language easy, free, and polished; but we cannot allow them strength of mind, deep reasoning powers, nor, in every instance, that firm solid judgment found in the other sex."[11]

The fact that male critics failed to take women writers seriously did not influence women readers. Women constituted three-fourths of the total reading public, and the novel was particularly satisfying to them because the characters were often familiar. Fiction gave women an opportunity to participate vicariously in other people's lives, and thus constituted a relief from their dull, routine existence. Furthermore, without sacrificing its stereotyped presentation of women, the novel treated all social classes, even though most of the women authors were middle class. Most readers also came from the increasingly affluent middle class. (As in any situation, however, there were exceptions. A few upper-class women, such as the Duchess of Devonshire and Lady Craven, wrote novels, as well as Ann Yearsley, the Bristol milkwoman who was discussed in chapter 2.)

Not all novels, however, were purchased by individuals. Reading clubs and lending libraries circulated novels. Working-class girls were exposed to novels—exemplary ones, of course — through the Sunday school classes that they attended. Moreover, the novel, for better or worse, was becoming respectable, and reviews were beginning to appear in magazines and newspapers. The *Ladies Monthly Museum* of 1798 featured a monthly review of "female literature," and the *Quarterly Review*, despite the fact that it barred women from its writing staff, reviewed novels by Fanny Burney, Mary Russell Mitford, Jane Austen, Maria Edgeworth, Sydney Owenson Morgan, and Mary Shelley. *Blackwood's Edinburgh Magazine*, the *Critical Review*, and the *Monthly Mirror* also reviewed works by women, rarely voicing praise, but supplying at least some negative publicity. Actually, there were repercussions over the fact that fiction by women was reviewed at all. Byron, for instance, thought that women writers were so inconsequential that to review them, pro or con, was, in his estimate, superfluous. Protesting to John Murray, the publisher of the *Quarterly Review*, about the "nasty" reviews of Lady Morgan's novels, Bryon wrote: "What cruel work you make of Lady Morgan! You should recollect that she is a woman; though, to be sure, they are now and then very provoking; still as authoresses, they can do no great harm; and I think it a pity such good invective should have been laid out upon her, when there is such a fine field of us Jacobin gentlemen for you to work upon?"[12] Byron is a gentleman — and a male chauvinist — to the end.

Many women writers shared Byron's view. They harbored curiously negative self-images — aspects of which they occasionally revealed in their novels. "I would rather scrub floors [than write novels]," Mary Russell Mitford insisted, "if I could get as much [money] by the healthier, more respectful and more *feminine* employment."[13] In Amelia Opie's novel *Mother and Daughter*, Mrs. Mowbray "ceased to be contented with reading, and was eager to become a writer also. But, as she was strongly imbued with the prejudices of an ancient family, she could not think of disgracing that family by turning professed author." Thus, from Mary Russell Mitford's pithy utterance to

Mrs. Mowbray's lamentation, self-deprecation among females ran high.

The more famous women authors, simultaneously pleased with the sale of their novels and with their notoriety, also felt somewhat guilty because of their unladylike profession. Like the Scottish songstress Carolina Oliphant (Lady Nairn), they considered it "a disgrace for a woman 'to have ink on her thumb' when her hand was kissed."[14] In a letter to Alicia Lefanu, the sister of Richard Brinsley Sheridan, Lady Morgan defensively tried to dispel the image of herself as a blue-stocking. "I must tell you, my dear madam," she wrote,

I am *ambitious*, far, far beyond the line of
laudable emulation, perhaps beyond the power of being happy. Yet the strongest point of my ambition
is to be *every inch a woman*. Delighted with the
pages of *La Voisier*, I dropped the study of
chemistry, though urged to it by a favourite friend
and preceptor, lest I should be less the *woman*.
Seduced by taste, and a thousand arguments to Greek
and Latin, I resisted, lest I should not be a very
woman. And I have studied music rather as a sentiment than a science, and drawing as an amusement
rather than an *art*, lest I should have become a
musical *pedant* or a *masculine artist*. And let
me assure you, that if I admire you for any one thing
more than another, it is that, with all your talent
and information, you are "a woman still."[15]

Ann Radcliffe, her critics tell us, was "ashamed of her own talents, and was ready to sink into the earth at the bare suspicion of anyone's taking her for an authoress [since] her chief ambition. . .[was] to be thought a lady."[16]

The very fear of being thought of as a writer rather than as a lady (or as a gentleman, for that matter, in the case of male writers, for novels, perhaps because many were written by women, were not highly regarded at the time) caused some authors to publish their work, especially their early writings, anonymously or pseudonymously. Another reason for publishing anonymously was that publishers discriminated against women, and an unknown writer bearing a woman's name would have virtually no chance of seeing her work in print. Even Fanny Burney sought anonymity when she published her first novel, and wrote in her diary: "I am frightened out of my wits from the terror of being attacked *as an author*, and therefore *shirk*, instead of *seeking* all occasions of being drawn into notice."

Women writers, especially the more successful ones, perhaps because the profession carried little prestige and because they were so often criticized, were, with few exceptions, mutually supportive. Madame de Stael, for instance, wrote to Fanny Burney addressing her letter "a la première femme d'angleterre."[7] Maria Edgeworth, throughout her life, read and praised books written by other women. And when Mary Russell Mitford's father died, leaving her in considerable debt, not only did her friends and readers organize a fund for her, but other literary ladies such as Joanna Baillie, Maria Edgeworth, Frances Trollope, and Amelia Opie raised money to help her. These women — all of whom were of the upper middle class — formed an informal group and believed themselves to be somewhat above other middle- and lower-middle-class women writers, who they thought demonstrated, in writing, their greed rather than their sensibility.

However, such sexist support of needy women novelists did not necessarily extend to their books. Anna L. Barbauld, in the early nineteenth century, claimed that the novel demanded "no education beyond literacy" and offered "no higher reward than amusement." Jane West, whose books on women's education and child rearing have been discussed earlier, added: "Novels like stong wine, made young ladies giddy." Hannah More claimed that novels "are mischievous in a thousand." Vineta Colby, a modern critic, made essentially the same point, that novels were one-dimensional and not very important. She suggested that nearly the entire contents of women's novels written during the early nineteenth century centered on "bourgeois family life." Other domestic or exemplary novels featured women deviants who experienced a variety of alternatives alien to "bourgeois family life." Women also wrote regional narratives, descriptive works using dialect that featured characters from the peasant classes. Still others, the so-called Gothic or escapist novelists, concentrated on fantastic situations.

Although there is a difference in the types of novels that appeared and in the situations that they dramatized, most women characters were stereotypes: attractive, superficial, subordinate to men. Such novels, written by women, mainly for women, served to enforce society's sexist treatment of the female. Rather than trying to change society, women novelists sought not only to maintain its values but even to make their readers conform to them. The two genres considered here are the novel of manners and the regional narrative. In both, women are subordinate to men.

The most popular of the novels of manners and the first widely acclaimed novel written by a woman was Fanny Burney's *Evelina*, published in 1778. *Evelina* is a prototypical novel of manners. In defining this genre, Burney stated: "It ought to be a picture of supposed, but natural and probably human existence. It holds, therefore, in its hands our best affections; it exercises our imagination; it points out the path of honour; and gives to juvenile credulity knowledge of the world, without ruin or repentance; and the lessons of experience without its tears." This is as much a definition of Fanny's life as it is of her novels.

The writing of *Evelina* was "natural and probable." Fanny Burney's father held a doctorate in music, and in her own home Fanny had an opportunity to observe people from all classes of society. On the one hand, her father permitted her free intercourse with maids and butlers and, on the other, he gave her every opportunity of watching society at ease in the company of artists and men of letters. Fanny "exercised her imagination" by writing "The History of Carolyn Evelyn," which she burned shortly after completion because her stepmother considered writing a waste of time for young, marriageable

Fanny Burney
COURTESY OF THE NATIONAL PORTRAIT GALLERY, LONDON

women.[18] Shortly after, Fanny was again at work—more surreptitiously this time, for she had, like her heroines, learned "the lessons of experience without tears." She wrote on scraps of paper "in a feigned hand."[19] The result was *Evelina; or, The History of a Young Lady's Entrance into the World*. Her brother took the manuscript to a publisher, who bought it for twenty pounds. When the publisher sent the author's proofs, they were addressed to a Mr. Grafton at the Orange Coffee House, where the Burney boy picked them up.

When Lowndes, the publisher, was asked who the author of *Evelina* was, he answered that "he. . .was a gentleman. . .[who] was a master of his subject and well versed in the manners of the times."[20]

Evelina is an epistolary novel consisting mostly of Evelina's letters to her guardian, Mr. Villars, and his replies. Evelina learns to cultivate a sense of values, "to discriminate between what is lasting and worthy and what is transient and meaningless, not by the promptings of. . .[her] heart but by the discipline of. . .[her] mind, by the training of 'discretion' and 'thought'." She meets her pushy, affected relatives, the Branghtons and, after some embarrassing moments, she learns to discriminate between the upper and lower middle classes. Throughout her travels in society, to balls and to teas, Evelina reports her impressions to her guardian, and thus contemporary readers can derive a clear picture of woman's role in late-eighteenth-century society. Describing a private ball, for example, Evelina says that "the gentlemen, as they passed and repassed, looked as if they thought we were quite at their disposal and only waiting for the honour of their commands." She also quotes the comments of a Mr. Smith on marriage: " 'For, to be sure, marriage is all in all with the ladies; but with us gentlemen it's quite another thing.' " This is obviously a man's world, and when Evelina is finally proposed to by her favorite, Lord Orville, her mentor, Mrs. Selwyn, advises her "to marry him directly. . .[for] the young men of this age are not to be trusted with too much time for deliberation, where their interests are concerned."

Even Mr. Villars, Evelina's ostensibly liberated guardian, makes a subtle distinction between men and women. He tells Evelina that "though gentleness and modesty are the peculiar attributes of your sex, yet fortitude and firmness, when occasion demands them, are virtues as noble and as becoming in women as in men: the right line of conduct is the same for both sexes, though the manner in which it is pursued, may somewhat vary, and be accommodated to the strength or weakness of the different travellers." Evelina may be firm, but she must disguise the firmness.

Mr Villars' comment seems to sum up Evelina's life. She marries Lord Orville and will live happily ever after—pursuing the "right line of conduct." Hence, Evelina's social training is as instructive as it is entertaining, both for the young ladies who read about her life and for their mothers, grandmothers, and aunts. Its message is clear. If a young lady establishes good connections and behaves in a charming, chaste, and deferential manner, pursuing the "right line of conduct," she will marry a suitable man and consequently have a happy life.

Fanny Burney wrote three more novels after *Evelina*, but although she received more money for them, none was as successful. In 1782 she published *Cecilia; or, Memoirs of an Heiress*, which has a more intricate plot than *Evelina* but it was criticized for a prosiness said to be reminiscent of Dr. Johnson. The *Monthly Review* criticized its "particularly nervous style modeled on Dr. Johnson," and Horace Walpole claimed that *Camilla* (1796) was written in Dr. Johnson's "unnatural phrase." Her last two novels, *Camilla* and *The Wanderer* (1814), were poorly executed and tedious, but they were financial successes nevertheless since Fanny's reputation had been so well established by *Evelina*.

Fanny Burney also served a five-year stint as the Queen's dresser. As Catherine J. Hamilton ironically expressed it in her biography, "Because Miss Burney was the first female novelist of the day, she was therefore fitted to assist at the Queen's toilette; according to this argument, because a horse has won the Derby it is therefore fitted to draw turnips."[21]

Women's sphere was limited, but women could be fulfilled, suggested the female authors of the day, through a proper

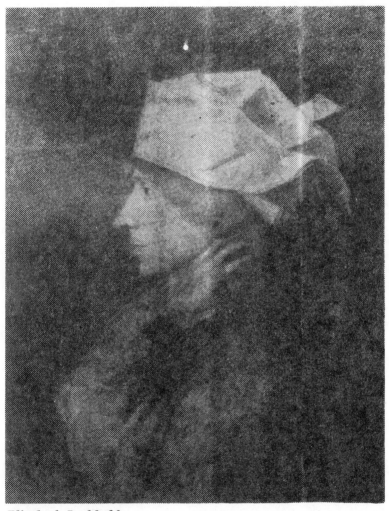

Elizabeth Inchbald
COURTESY OF THE NATIONAL PORTRAIT GALLERY, LONDON

education. Although Evelina was properly "educated" through her exposure to society, Miss Milner, the heroine of Elizabeth Inchbald's *A Simple Story* (1796), receives a frivolous education directed by her older guardian, Dorriforth, who is somewhat smitten by his young charge. He alternately indulges her and tests her — so that she turns into a "gay," "proud," and "haughty" young woman. When he attempts to change from permissive guardian to rigid husband Miss Milner is unchangeable.

Shortly before he is to marry Miss Milner, Dorriforth, who becomes Lord Elmwood, criticizes her "want of economy." "Bills and drafts came upon him without number, [while] the account, on her part, of money expended, amounted but to articles of dress she sometimes never wore, toys that were out of fashion before they were paid for, and charities directed by the force of whim."

Miss Milner's superficiality and pretentiousness are also evident in her behavior at an auction, where she buys items for which she has no use simply, "because they were said to be cheap." Mr. Sandford, Lord Elmwood's friend, notices a group of books on chemistry and Latin that she has purchased. "Why madam," he says, "do you know what you have done? You can't read a word of these books." And she answers: "Can't I, Mr. Sandford? but I assure you, you will be vastly pleased with them when you see how elegantly they are bound."

Nevertheless, Lord Elmwood marries her and in the third volume of the novel the deterioration of the once lovely and innocent Lady Elmwood is described. "The beautiful, the beloved Miss Milner," Elizabeth Inchbald melodramatically informs the reader, "is no longer beautiful — no longer beloved — no longer — tremble while you read it! — no longer — virtuous." Consequently, Lord Elmwood becomes an implacable tyrant who refuses to see his only daughter "in vengeance to her mother's crimes."

The author then backtracks to explain that while Lord Elmwood was in the West Indies, Lady Elmwood, quite bored, began "mixing in the gayest circles in London" and then took a lover. Lord Elmwood returns, his love for his wife turns to hate, and Lady Elmwood dies with two-thirds of volume three still remaining.

Although Maria Edgeworth, who greatly admired Inchbald's novel and agreed with her in attributing Miss Milner's demise to the lack of "a proper education," which resulted in a "charming, accomplished young woman. . .who lack[ed] the strength of character necessary for a prudent life,"[22] it seems that no matter what kind of an education women received in the late eighteenth and early nineteenth century, it was often the emptiness and futility of their lives that caused them to become unfaithful.

The rest of the novel is devoted to the stricter, more piously oriented upbringing of Matilda, the daughter of Lord and Lady Elmwood, who is finally reconciled with her father and marries her suitor, Rushbrook, a distant relative and her father's heir, presumably to live happily ever after. This difference in upbringing of mother and daughter coincides with the general middle-class revolt against regency and eighteenth-century frivolity and looseness. In the nineteenth century, the rising middle class was becoming strict and moralistic.

The contrast between Matilda's placidity and her mother's volubility, and between some of the more melodramatic events in the narrative, such as Matilda's meeting with her father, may be attributed to Elizabeth Inchbald's early career as an actress and playwright. *A Simple Story* was published twelve years after it was written and only then because of its author's reputation as an actress. Just as Fanny Burney's literary fame was hardly a suitable qualification for her becoming a Queen's dresser, Elizabeth Inchbald's acting ability did not necessarily equip her to be a novelist.

Young girls such as Evelina underwent a proper socialization in order to marry well. But somehow, as Inchbald indicates through the character of Lady Elmwood, a so-called proper marriage did not always bring happiness. The circumstance of women's boredom with their domestic situation appears again in Maria Edgeworth's *Belinda*, (1801). A long, panoramic novel with several subplots, this work focuses on two characters who are, in a sense, foils. Belinda, literary cousin to Evelina, is a young girl sent by her aunt to live with a sophisticated gadabout, Lady Delacour. But as the story progresses, Belinda becomes more of an influence on Lady Delacour than Lady Delacour is on her. (Here, the hourglass device that Henry James was to utilize a century later is already at work.)

Belinda touches on all upper-middle-class women's concerns — morality, education, responsibility, the contrast between a merely beautiful female and a beautiful and accomplished female, the plight of the single woman, and others. Although Maria Edgeworth remained unmarried all her life, she realized that her situation, that of living in a huge house with many brothers and sisters, nieces, and nephews, whom she could both write for and teach, was an uncommon one, and throughout the novel she still seems to advocate marriage as the only desirable goal for young ladies.

Early in the novel, Belinda's aunt, Mrs. Stanhope, explains to her niece that "a young lady's chief business is to please in society, that all her charms and accomplishments should be invariably subservient to one grand object — establishing herself in the world," that is, making a proper marriage, and she warns Belinda of the unhappy consequences of failing to find a husband. "Nothing," Mrs. Stanhope says, "can be more miserable than the situation of a poor girl, who, after spending not only the interest, but the solid capital of her small fortune in dress and frivolous extravagance, fails in her matrimonial expectations. . .she finds herself at five- or six- and thirty a burden to her friends, destitute of the means of rendering herself independent."

Yet Lady Delacour's domestic situation, as we first see it, hardly presents an argument for marriage. She is erratic: "Abroad she appeared all life, spirit, and good humour — at home, listless, fretful, and melancholy." She neglects her only daughter, as well as her husband, who takes to drink in her absence. She taunts him at every opportunity, viciously telling Belinda in his presence, for instance, that "he can drink more than any two-legged animal in his majesty's dominons." And that, she adds, "is an advantage which is well worth twenty or thirty years of a man's life—especially to persons who have no chance of distinguising themselves."

Actually, most of the men in *Belinda* are weak. Clarence Hervey, Belinda's principal suitor, possesses a "chameleon character," for "he could be all things to all men—and to all women." A friend of his, a venerable doctor, pities him, as "a man who might be anything. . .[but who] choose[s] to be—nothing."

Perhaps Maria Edgeworth is implying that, given the opportunity, an intelligent woman would not waste her life. Or perhaps she is indicating, as seems more likely, that, in order for a man to be successful, he needs to be married to a dedicated woman, a true helpmate. Clarence eventually marries Belinda after she has helped him to find a purposeful existence. Similarly, after Lady Delacour's critical illness, when she decides to finally concentrate on seeking domestic happiness, her husband becomes a happier, stable man.

Belinda meets some of the same social types as Evelina—the superficial woman, "one of those ladies who can remember or forget people, be perfectly familiar or stangely rude, just as it suits the convenience, fashion, or humour of the minute." She also hears about an innocent girl who is kidnapped from boarding school by a scoundrel (echoes of Hannah More's Clementina), whose daughter, raised by her grandmother (the mother has died of a broken heart) meets, by coincidence, Clarence Hervey.

Page upon page is devoted to the story of the innocent young girl, whom her grandmother is determined to bring up and shelter from the evils of society. Imagine the quandary of young readers of the day: on the one hand, they were urged to find husbands—or else, and, on the other, there were so many tales in circulation about girls who got the "wrong" husbands. It seemed to be a situation where either girls got husbands to *use*, for support and respectability, or else men got girls, mistresses, or wives, whom *they* used for sex or money and then discarded.

Clarence, however, is intrigued by the innocent Virginia, especially by her "sensibility," that is, her naiveté, impressionism, and delicacy, all much-favored nineteenth-century virtues. He observes the difference between Virginia, a "child of nature," and the "frivolous, sophisticated slaves of art." To test her — throughout literature, it seems, maidens are tested — he asks her to choose a rose or a pair of diamond earrings. Naturally, she chooses the rose, but, in comparison with Belinda, Virginia appears "an insipid, though innocent child." Belinda, he realizes, would be "a companion, a friend to him for life." Virginia would be only "his pupil or plaything." One wonders what, in real life, the man's choice would actually be.

But what about broken-hearted Virginia? In a melodramatic scene echoing the one in Elizabeth Inchbald's *A Simple Story* in which Matilda first sees her estranged father, Virginia meets her own father after thirteen years and plans to devote her life to making him happy. It seems not to matter whether it is a husband, father, or brother. As long as a woman devotes her life to a man, she is fulfilling her role. Like *Evelina*, the novel concludes with the impending marriage of Belinda and Clarence.

In contrast, Susan Ferrier's *Marriage, a Novel* (1818) begins with a marriage, but, it is suggested, a marriage entered into for the wrong reasons. Characteristically, the heroine must pay for her mistake. Early in the novel, Juliana, the heroine, is told by her father, who wants her to marry an old, ugly, but very rich duke, that "she shall marry for the purpose for which matrimony was ordained amongst people of birth — that is, for the aggrandisement of her family, the extending of their political influence, — for becoming, in short, the depository of their mutual interest. These are the only purposes [for] which persons of rank ever think of marriage."

Juliana defies her father and, instead, elopes with her lover, a handsome young Scot, and they go to live with his gregarious but drearily middle-class family. The theme that one cannot live on love alone is implicit, for the spoiled Juliana, who cannot adjust to Henry's family, is miserable. Juliana is neither a social lioness like Edgeworth's Lady Delacour nor a sensible woman with interests like Belinda or Evelina. She is of the upper class and has been taught — more correctly, trained — by her father (her mother is never mentioned) to be idle. She is, then, both spoiled and bored. In fact, as Vineta Colby suggests, the novel might "accurately have been titled '*Education*,' for its theme is the effect of childhood conditioning and training upon character."²³

Juliana is, for example, even unable to dress without a maid's help. "I never did such [an impossible] thing in my life," she despairs. She is unable to entertain herself except by dancing or playing cards; she is jealous of, and hence neglects, her twin daughters. She shortly comes to rue her marital decision and tells her husband that she might find the old Duke whom her father wanted her to marry handsome now. "People's tastes alter according to circumstances," she explains. Henry humorously retorts: "Yours must have undergone a wonderful revolution, if you can find charms in a hunchback of fifty-three." "He is not a hunchback," returns her Ladyship warmly; "only a little high shouldered, but at any rate he has the most beautiful place and the finest house in England!"

If Lady Juliana's husband is somewhat irate at his wife's change of heart, his father is even less tolerant of her whims. " 'Edication,' says he. . .'if a woman can nurse her bairns, mak' their claes, and manage her hoose, what mair need she do? If she can play a tune on the spinnet, and dance a reel, and play a rubber at whist — nae doot these are accomplishments.' "

Through Juliana, Susan Ferrier reveals yet another significant aspect of early-nineteenth-century women's behavior — specifically, the upper-class indifference toward the lower echelons of society. Lady Juliana's curiosity is aroused when she sees her sister-in-law, Mrs. Douglas, knitting children's stockings. When Mrs. Douglas explains that she has no children of her own, Juliana asks her why she makes them. "I make them for those whose parents cannot afford to purchase them," Mrs. Douglas replies. "What poor wretches they must be, that can't afford to buy stockings," explains Juliana. "It's monstrous good of you to make them, to be sure; but it must be a shocking bore! and such a trouble!" Mrs. Douglas, nevertheless, has the last word. "Not half such a bore," she retorts, "as you undergo with your favourites [Juliana's miniature pet dogs]." Mrs. Douglas is obviously a foil. She does what a good woman ought to do, and thereby reveals the badness of Juliana.

Similarly, in volume 2, Juliana's niece describes an odious upper-class woman who finds "nothing so degrading as associating with our inferiors—that is, our inferiors in rank and wealth. . .with the lower orders of society she is totally unacquainted; she knows they are meanly clothed and coarsely fed, consequently they are mean."

Ultimately, Juliana leaves her husband and her Scottish home to return to London to live with her brother, Lord Lindore, a wealthy man whose wife has run off with a servant, a kind of reversal of Juliana's situation. The implication, it seems, is that neither love nor money can bring fulfillment to the sheltered, superficially educated, bored, nineteenth-century woman.

Volume 2 of *Marriage* concentrates on the lives of Lady Juliana's two daughters. Adelaide lives with her upper-class mother in England, and Mary is brought up by her middle-class aunt, Mrs. Douglas, in Scotland. Adelaide, the image of her mother, Juliana, who considers herself a "victim" of love and who thus desires to save her daughter from the same "error," marries for money and to please her mother—but she finds the man despicable. She eventually leaves him and elopes with her lover, a cousin she has always loved.

Mary, on the other hand, receives her "education" from her Scottish aunts. Susan Ferrier humorously dramatizes their opinions. "I'm certain—indeed, I think there's no doubt of it," says Miss Grizzy, "that reading does young people much harm. It puts things into their heads that never would have been there but for books. I declare, I think reading's a very dangerous thing. . . ." " 'Much depends upon the choice of books,' said Jacky, with an air of the most profound wisdom. *'Fordyce's Sermons* and the *History of Scotland* are two of the very few books *I* would put into the hands of a young woman.' "

The important ingredient in Mary's education, however, an element lacking in Adelaide's, relates to character. Mary learns to be kind, generous, and tolerant. At eighteen, when she goes to visit her sister and mother in London, she receives a profound shock, for she perceives the difference between her values and those of the upper classes. Once again, the theme of the moral superiority of the emerging middle class, especially Scottish Calvinists, is obvious.

The Londoners stress material things and the Scots are more concerned with people. For example, Adelaide tells her sister, Mary, shortly after she has arrived: "You will. . .be at no loss for amusement; you will find musical instruments there. . .and here are new publications, and *portefeuilles* of drawings you will perhaps like to look over!" She never thinks of keeping Mary company, however, despite not having seen her sister for years.

Emily, Mary's cousin, moreover, berates the vacuity of the upper-class female. "Married ladies," she says, are "only celebrated for their good dinners, or their pretty equipages, or their fine jewels. How I should scorn to be talked of as the appendage to any soups or pearls!" Having indicted the mothers, Emily attacks the "insipidity" of their daughters — "Misses, who are mere misses, and nothing more. . .with pretty hair and fashionable clothes; — *sans* eyes for anything but lovers — *sans* ears for anything but flattery — *sans* taste for anything but balls — *sans* brains for anything at all."

Although the action deteriorates in the second volume, the friendship between Mary and her cousin Emily is beautifully depicted, which was rare for that period, when women in novels were usually in competition. Mary and Emily, from different backgrounds, are, nevertheless, considerate and mutually supportive — they are not striving for a man's attentions — and truly attempt to understand each other's feelings. Their conversations give Ferrier an opportunity to inject many of her own views on women and society. Unfortunately, the emptiness of the lives of rich upper-class women and frivolous young girls is presented, it seems, more for the sake of entertainment than as protest. Nevertheless, male reviewers found Ferrier's criticism of superficial, frivolous, and subservient females objectionable. The reviewer of *Marriage* in *Blackwood's Edinburgh Magazine* praises women authors such as Maria Edgeworth and Fanny Burney for their depiction of "the minutiae of social life," and for their "intimate acquaintance with the characters of women," but he calls Susan Ferrier a "spy" for "babbling 'the secrets of the prison-house' most unconscionably."[24] Although the reviewer also criticizes both the length of the book and its diffuseness, he generally approves of the subject of women's lives as an acceptable topic for women writers. Male reviewers did not want women's subordinate role criticized — even indirectly.

A second category of novels dealing with the trials of domestic life falls broadly into two groups — the purely regional work, portraying peasant life, and other works focusing on women who deviate from society's rules. Four novels represent the first group: *The Cottagers of Glenburnie*, a Scottish story written by Elizabeth Hamilton in 1808; *The Wild Irish Girl* (1806), by Sydney Owenson Morgan; *Our Village*, by Mary Russell Mitford, set in rural England and published serially between 1824 and 1832; and *Castle Rackrent*, by Maria Edgeworth, set in Ireland and published in 1800.

Although Susan Ferrier's *Marriage*, a novel of manners, is partly set in Scotland and re-creates the middle-class Scots' dialect, it is primarily concerned with depicting the life-style of an upper-class woman, as well as the socialization of the woman's young daughters. The four regional novels focus more on the life-style of a group, usually the lower class.

The first three novels, *The Cottagers of Glenburnie, Our Village,* and *The Wild Irish Girl,* are inferior to *Castle Rackrent* in narrative presentation and characterization, but since they reinforced society's views of woman's role, they were more acceptable to the male critics than was *Castle Rackrent.*

Elizabeth Hamilton, whose best known works were on education, remained a spinster, adopting the title of *Mrs.* in middle age. Her father was a clergyman; her mother had died in childbirth. From the age of eight to thirteen she attended a seminary school. At thirteen she stayed home, and her aunt engaged a friend to assist her progress in music and drawing.

She believed that marriage and a husband took possession of a woman's life. Lamenting the loss of a close friend, she said: "My friend Miss C——'s marriage has deprived me of both sisters." (Her real sister had married a few years before.)

Women writers, no matter how talented or successful, had to be apologized for, and Elizabeth Hamilton was no exception. A close friend of hers stated that she alleviated the "vulgar prejudices against literary women. . .by extending the sphere of female usefulness," adding that "she did a great amount of charity work for children and their poor parents."

The Cottagers of Glenburnie is a semiautobiographical, didactic work, for Hamilton wanted to educate the reader on how to live. Mrs. Mason, the narrator and Hamilton's spokeswoman, explains how she has devoted her life to living with relatives and friends in an effort to teach them to live better.

First she stays with two sisters (she had been a friend of their late mother), one sensible, the other frivolous. Explains the sensible girl to Mrs. Mason: "My father wishes us always to be dressed according to our station and I think it a pity such notions should ever be out of fashion." Since women were usually judged strictly on the basis of appearance, females, even more than males, in England's rigid society, should, of course, know their place—and, through clothing, indicate it.

Mrs. Mason accepts a position as a seamstress with an upperclass family. Her most heroic effort occurs when she saves every

one of her employers from a fire started by a careless servant—who is burned to death, the only victim of the conflagra-
tion. For her heroism, Mrs. Mason is elevated to the post of
governess, with a salary of thirty pounds per year. The implication for the time was that life for a lower-middle-class woman
could be rewarding if she was pious, honest, and dedicated,
and, above all else, if she knew her place.

Speaking about her charges, Mrs. Mason typically makes
male-female distinctions: "The young ladies so graceful, so
sweet-tempered, and so accomplished! and the young
gentlemen so well behaved, and at the same time so clever,
that all their masters said, they learned better and faster than
any scholars they had." In early-nineteenth-century England,
women were "accomplished," but men were "clever."

When the children grow up, Mrs. Mason, who still has years
of usefulness left, goes to live with distant relatives, the Mc-
Clartys, cottagers at Glenburnie. Their ignorance is intrac-
table, and they suffer continually for their failure to heed Mrs.
Mason's advice and simple maxims. For example, when a Mc-
Clarty child refuses to attend school and Mrs. Mason
reprimands her, the mother sides with the child. "If you permit
your daughter, while a child, to disobey her parent and her
teacher, she will never learn to obey God," responds Mrs.
Mason, but her warning is in vain.

When Mr. McClarty falls ill, his wife refuses to listen to Mrs.
Mason's pleas to call a doctor and to give him fresh air. Instead, she takes the advice of her ignorant neighbors. Mr. Mc-
Clarty dies, and his wife and son contract the same illness.
Completely disgusted, but never despairing—for virtuous
nineteenth-century Christian ladies never capitulated—Mrs.
Mason goes to live with another family, the Morrisons. The
contrast between these two families makes for rather dull
reading, but it gave Hamilton further opportunity to reveal her
many views on education, particularly its influence on the
lower-class woman in her home.

Mrs. Mason prepares the Morrisons' daughters for life when
she tells them that "in order to make good servants," they have

only to attend to three simple rules: "Do everything in its proper time; keep everything to its proper use; and put everything in its proper place." Working-class women and daughters of cottagers were destined to be domestic servants. The only choice they had was whether to be efficient or derelict in their duties.

As for the ignorant McClarty family, the author has Mrs. Mason explain what happened, lest the reader have any doubt about the certainty of irreligious people's coming to a bad end. Mrs. McClarty's son is "tricked" into marriage by the daughter of a smuggler. His mother is violently opposed, and so her son, now head of the household, turns her out—an incident that shows how few rights women had. Although a wife may have taken care of her husband's home for years, the eldest son became its owner upon his father's death. Mrs. McClarty then goes to live with her daughters, both of whom earn adequate salaries working in muslin factories. In "their vanity and pride," they spend all their earnings on "finery." One girl becomes involved with a workman who deserts her; she bears his child, leaves it with her mother, and goes to Edinburgh, never to be heard from again. The other daughter's conduct is not quite so bad, but Mrs. Mason explains: "Her notions of duty were not such as to afford much comfort to her mother's heart." In contrast, the Morrison girls take over a little school where their father is headmaster—they teach needlework, as Mrs. Mason had done—and Mrs. Mason takes possession of a cottage built for her by her former employer, Lord Langlands. It is in this "sweet retreat" that "she tranquilly spent the last days of a useful life."

The people who crowd the canvas of Mary Russell Mitford's *Our Village* come from essentially the same social class as the Glenburnie cottagers. But Mitford's treatment of her regional characters differs from Elizabeth Hamilton's. The settting is often emphasized at the expense of characterization. When the emphasis is on character—specifically, on that of the lower-class woman—Mitford is quite sympathetic, provided that the character knows her place. In a vignette concerning a woman

named Hannah, a widow with two young daughters, the narrator states: "Cast thus upon the world, there must have been
much to endure, much to suffer." Mitford's narrator also
praises Hannah's fortitude. Hannah, she tells us, whose trials
were "borne with a smiling patience, a hopeful cheeriness of
spirit and a decent pride, seemed to command success as well
as respect in [her] struggle for independence." Hannah maintains herself and her daughters by needlework and by washing
and mending fine linens.

When working-class women attempted to emulate their
middle-class sisters by displaying an interest in finery, however,
they were sharply reprimanded. The narrrator criticizes two
young women who "teach little children their ABCs [but also]
make caps and gowns for their mammas. . .[because] they find
adorning the body a more profitable vocation than adorning
the mind." Echoing Elizabeth Hamilton's criticism of the vain
McClarty girls in *The Cottagers of Glenburnie*, the narrator
describes her landlord's daughter: she is "all curl-papers in the
afternoon, like a poodle, with more flounces than curl-papers,
and more lovers than curls."

Mary Russell Mitford also supports society's view that the
diligent, uncomplaining poor will be rewarded. She tells about
a poor parish boy who rises by dint of manual labor to the rank
of landowner, and about a poor, motherless, but virtuous and
industrious girl who manages to run a prosperous farm
(presumably her late father's) and is subsequently rewarded by
being wooed and wed by a handsome neighbor. A man is
rewarded by his profession; a woman, by her marriage.

One would think that with all Mitford's sentimentality and
reinforcement of society's values, she would have been lauded
by her reviewers. Although the critics praised her poignant
descriptions of nature and humble folk, they vehemently objected to her clever use of dialect, what they called "low and
provincial corruptions of language," that is, her use of words
such as "rolypoly," "dumpiness," "pot-luck," and "hurry-
scurry."[25] One reviewer claimed that he would have better enjoyed Mrs. Mitford had she been "less ambitious of astonishing

us male creatures by her acquaintance with the mysteries of cricketing and coursing."[26] These were sacred male preserves, evidently.

Mary Russell Mitford
COURTESY OF THE NATIONAL PORTRAIT GALLERY, LONDON

The reviewer further criticized a colorful description of a kennel of greyhounds in *Our Village*. The passage, he asserted, is "strangely unbecoming [to] a female mouth."[27] The author refers to the offspring of Hector, a superb greyhound as "little bitches," "excellently loined," and "chested like war-horses." She also describes how a female hare killed one of the dogs (presumably a male).[28]

There is no doubt that contemporary reviewers applied a double standard in evaluating novels written by women and those by men. In the case of Sydney Owenson, later Lady Morgan, her third and most famous novel, *The Wild Irish Girl*, is inferior artistically to her three subsequent novels. But Glorvina, "the wild Irish girl," is a subordinate character in the novel, as well as a subordinate female in contrast to the more aggressive and substantial heroines of the later novels. Probably for this reason, Morgan's reputation as a female novelist rests primarily on *The Wild Irish Girl*.

Sydney Owenson Morgan grew up in the intellectual tradition of Fanny Burney and Maria Edgeworth. Her father was an actor, and "Shakespeare, Handel, and Carolan, the Irish bard, were the three *Dii Majorum Gentium* of our household altars," said Morgan in later years.[29] She received a "proper education"—that is, she attended a finishing school of sorts that was known for its "strictness of discipline"—briefly worked as a governess, and then published, with her father's help, a volume of poems.[30] That was followed in 1802 by a novel set in Ireland, *St. Clair*, and a second novel, *The Novice*, depicting "the historical background of France at the end of the sixteenth century."[31]

To prepare for writing *The Wild Irish Girl*, Morgan visited many parts of Ireland, studied Irish history and archaeology, and spoke to experts on Irish poetry, politics and customs. The result, as her biographer, Lionel Stevenson, notes, is that "many pages of her books were occupied more by footnotes than by text."[32] Published in 1806, *The Wild Irish Girl* is, like *Evelina*, epistolary. A young Englishman, Mortimer, who is banished by his father to the latter's Irish estates, meets a beautiful, simple girl, Glorvina, whose father, a descendant of the original lords of the region, continues to reside in a ruinous castle and calls himself the "prince of Inishmore." Mortimer poses as an artist and, as the story unfolds, he falls in love with Glorvina, with her father, with their wise old priest, and, most of all, with Ireland. Mortimer unhappily discovers that Glorvina is betrothed. Indeed, the man she is to marry is his own father, but at the very last moment Mortimer manages to secure Glorvina's hand. This odd triangle caused one critic to

Sydney Owenson Morgan
COURTESY OF THE NATIONAL PORTRAIT GALLERY, LONDON

call the book "a curious mixture of pedantry and melodrama," a "lengthy dissertation on Irish history and customs [that is] combined with a highly romantic love story."[33]

Morgan gives a complete historical background of Ireland and focuses on the prevailing class system. She explains, for instance, that "in Dublin the buildings are not arranged upon. . . democratic principles. The plebeian hut offers no foil to the patrician edifice." Still commenting on the class system, she tells how an intelligent peasant boy can raise his status — by becoming a priest. She also explains the class arrangement of the ancient Milefian government in Ireland, indicating how everyone knew his place — from "the princes to the peasant."

Yet women, regardless of class, were thought of, and therefore treated, as second-class citizens. Mortimer makes several comments on women that suggest this — particularly about English women, in contrast to Glorvina, the Irish lass whom he obviously prefers. He remarks how natural Glorvina is. "Hitherto," he explains, "I have only met servile copies, sketched by the finger of art, and finished off by the polished touch of fashion." He then comments on heroines of English novels. "Though they are the most perfect of beings, they are also the most stupid. Surely virtue would not be the less attractive for being united to genius and the graces."

What Mortimer, and Morgan, did not understand, however, is that women were not taught to be independent, to cultivate "genius." Consider the Prince of Inishmore's comment to Mortimer. "How delightful," he exclaims, "to form this young and ductile mind [of a woman], to mould it to your desires, to breathe inspiration into this lovely image of primeval innocence, to give soul to beauty, and intelligence to simplicity, to watch the ripening progress of your grateful efforts and finally clasp to your heart that perfection you have yourself created." If, as the prince suggests, women were mere flowers to be cultivated, naturally they would wither quickly.

In subsequent novels, Morgan gives a more prominent role to her female characters. In *Florence McCarthy, Ida of Athens,* and *O'Donnell* the central characters are women, and, Stevenson claims, in *Ida of Athens* Morgan "defended her own sex in a man-dominated world."[34]

In *The Wild Irish Girl*, Morgan combines what Oliver Elton calls "a young-ladyish plot" with "a vindication of the Irish people, and especially the Irish poor as well as the landscape, song, and stories of her country."[35] Maria Edgeworth's regional novel, *Castle Rackrent*, on the other hand, is an indictment of the decadent Irish rich, and the plot is hardly "young-ladyish."

By presenting the story in the form of a memoir that is related to the narrator by an old Irish servant, Thady Quirk, Edgeworth captures the authentic Irish dialect, a clever feat. Thady explains how the original Irish landowners lost their land and money over three generations as a result of dissipation and mismanagement. Thus the reader can observe, without moral comment from the author, the ignominious demise of an effete aristocracy.

The women in *Castle Rackrent*, although minor characters, are strong and self-willed. And, what is unusual for the time since so many women died in childbirth or from tuberculosis, the women always seem to outlast the men. When her penny-pinching husband dies in a fit of temper, Lady Murtagh strips Castle Rackrent of its treasures and goes to London. Her brother-in-law, Kit, gets the estate and, in an effort to pay off the mortgage, marries a rich Jewess, whom he incarcerates in her room for seven years. When she is supposedly on her deathbed, Kit begs her to leave her jewels to him, but she refuses. Suddenly he is killed in a duel, and Lady Kit, just as suddenly, recovers and returns to her native London. Sir Condy, a distant cousin of Kit's, takes over the tottering estate, and he and his extravagant wife get into even greater debt when Sir Condy dies from gluttony. Then Jason, the thrifty son of Thady, the narrator, gets the estate and marries a fortune-hunting widow.

Castle Rackrent is considered by modern critics to be Maria Edgeworth's finest work. It is a kind of prototype of the Irish novel and it is "the first regional novel in English."[36] In addition, it provided the inspiration for *Waverly*, which Walter Scott began in 1805 and published in 1814. It is also the only novel that Edgeworth wrote without her father's help, and it generated a fair amount of critical debate. When women writers departed from the female stereotype, they were often harshly criticized. The *Quarterly Review*, for instance, castigated Edgeworth for a lack of decorum and for what they considered her audacity in writing like a man. Referring to Edgeworth's dialogue, the reviewer said: "Such conversation may doubtless be expected from coachmen and footmen, but does not deserve to be recorded by the pen of Miss Edgeworth."[37] The critic in the *Monthly Review, or Literary Journal* even condemned Edgeworth's *Belinda*, certainly a work more genteel than *Castle Rackrent*, and claimed that he preferred Maria Edgeworth on the subjects of morals and education. Women's role, the critics believed, was to preach morals, not to analyze character. Preaching morals is what most women writers tried to do—even though they often confused preaching with characterization.

While most women writers were ignored by men, some were tolerated, provided that they stuck to so-called women's topics. When they deviated from these subjects—or attempted to expand their interests—they were taken to task.

NOTES

1. Clara Reeve, *The Progress of Romance* (1785; reprint ed., New York: Facsimile Text Society, 1930), p. 111.

2. Review of *The Letters of Mrs. Elizabeth Montagu*, Part the Second, vols. 3, 4, pp. 31-41 in *Quarterly Review* 10, no. 19 (October 1813): 34.

3. Vineta Colby, *Yesterday's Woman: Domestic Realism in the English Novel* (Princeton, N.J.: Princeton University Press, 1974), p. 97.

4. Wilbur Cross, *The Development of the English Novel* (New York: Macmillan Co., 1900), p. 78.

5. George L. Barnett, ed., *Eighteenth Century British Novelists on the Novel* (New York: Appleton-Century-Crofts, 1968), p. 142.

6. Ernest A. Baker, *A History of the English Novel*, 11 vols. (London: Witherby, 1924), 5:107.

7. Eliza Parsons, *Mysterious Warnings* (1796; reprint ed., London: Folio Press, 1968), p. xvii.

8. *Monthly Magazine* (February 1789), quoted in Joyce Marjorie Sanxter Tompkins, *The Popular Novel in England, 1770-1800* (London: Constable & Co., 1932), p. 118 n.

9. *Quarterly Review* 10, no. 19 (October 1813): 31.

10. Ibid. 4, no. 514 (November 1810): 517

11. *Critical Review* 2, no. 4 (August 1804): 458.

12. Quoted in Lionel Stevenson, *The Wild Irish Girl: The Life of Sydney Owenson, Lady Morgan, 1776-1859* (London: Chapman & Hall, 1936), p. 189.

13. Quoted in Reginald Brimley Johnson, *The Women Novelists* (London: W. Collins Sons & Co., 1918), p. 141. Italics added.

14. Catherine J. Hamilton, *Women Writers: Their Works and Ways*, 1st ser. (1892; reprint ed., New York: Books for Libraries Press, 1971), p. 137.

15. Stevenson, *Wild Irish Girl*, pp. 58-59.

16. Hamilton, *Women Writers*, p. 150.

17. Ibid., p. 20.

18. Muriel Masefield, *Women Novelists from Fanny Burney to George Eliot* (London: I. Nicholson & Watson, 1934), p. 12, and Hamilton, *Women Writers*, p. 5.

19. Fanny Burney, *Evelina; or, The History of a Young Lady's Entrance into the World*, ed. Edward A. Bloom (London: Oxford University Press, 1968), p. xxiv.

20. Masefield, *Women Novelists*, p. 13.

21. Hamilton, *Women Writers*, p. 16.

22. Colby, *Yesterday's Woman*, p. 109.

23. Ibid., p. 102.

24. *Blackwood's Edinburgh Magazine* 3, no. 15 (June 1818): 286.

25. *Quarterly Review* 31, no. 166 (December 1824): 167.

26. Ibid.

27. Ibid.

28. Pierce Egan's *Life in London; or, The Day and Night Scenes of Jerry Hawthorne, Esq. and His Elegant Friend Corinthian Tom, Accompanied by Bob Logic, the Oxonian, in Their Rambles and Sprees through the Metropolis, 1821-28,* which reproduces the slang and cockneyisms of Londoners and is spiced with puns and wordplay, was praised by critics. In fact, Egan's style was later emulated by Charles Dickens in *The Pickwick Papers.* Ernest Baker and James Packman, *A Guide to the Best Fiction, English and American* (London: Routledge, 1932), p. 162.

29. Stevenson, *Wild Irish Girl*, p. 7.

30. Ibid., pp. 32-45.

31. Ibid., p. 64.

32. Ibid., p. 71.

33. Mona Wilson, *These Were Muses* (London: Sidgwick, 1924), pp. 70-71.

34. Stevenson, *Wild Irish Girl*, p. 111.

35. Oliver Elton, *A Survey of English Literature, 1770-1830*, 2 vols. (London: E. Arnold, 1924), 1:368.

36. Maria Edgeworth, *Castle Rackrent*, ed. George Watson (1800; reprint ed., London: Macmillan & Co., 1964), p. vii.

37. *Quarterly Review* 17, no. 34 (April 1817): 103.

6
Guilt, Expiation, and Escape: Fallen Women, Pious Ladies, and Gothic Heroines

I would at any time of my youth rather have been a heroine of romance than a celebrated authoress.

—Mary Martha Butt Sherwood

Most of the heroines discussed in the previous chapter got properly married to very proper men — the best thing that could happen to a nineteenth-century woman — according to the fiction. Not all of the female characters treated in this chapter fare as well. A mistress who bears an illegitimate child; a young orphan girl whose reputation is ruined by her conspiring landlady and an evil captain; a defiant young woman who lives with her lover and shuns marriage; and a repentant divorcée — these are the fictional characters of the so-called domestic and exemplary novels to be described in this chapter. The ladies composing this unfortunate quartet, each of whom is involved in specific trials of domestic life, suffer and are punished mainly because they defy an archaic, moralistic, and hypocritical society — a society that few, even among the more enlightened and intelligent women writers of the time, sought to change.

The third and final category to be considered is the Gothic novel. Artistically superior to manneristic and domestic — regional as well as exemplary — fiction, the Gothic novel was a heartier genre. Even today, Gothic novels are read, studied and imitated. Nevertheless, the Gothic novel featured stereotyped female characters — beautiful, passive, and suffering, perfectly pure or perfectly repentant. Male critics — especially those who reviewed exemplary or Gothic novels by women accidentally (when works were published anonymously, such as Mary Shelley's *Frankenstein*) or condescendingly — generally praised the portrayal of women as subordinate characters.

Amelia Alderson Opie exemplifies the statement that "only if a woman was fortunate enough to be born into an intellectual and liberal family could she utilize her writing talents." Fanny Burney's father was a music scholar; Maria Edgeworth's, a politician and writer; Sydney Owenson Morgan's, a famous actor; and Amelia Alderson's, a surgeon. Dr. Alderson indulged his daughter's every whim and did not subject her to a rigorous education, either secular or religious. She did not attend church regularly; her only formal learning consisted of "a few scraps of music and French." As Catherine J. Hamilton, one of her biographers, explains, Amelia Opie "grew up free from prejudice," sympathetic to the poor and needy, and with a yearning "for romance and adventure." The difference between Opie's experience and that of her heroines, Hamilton continues, "is sometimes difficult to reconcile." "Cheerful and sunshiny by nature, happy, loving, and beloved, with no rubs of fortune to contend against, Mrs. Opie's books are, as a rule, full of sadness and desolation, oppressed with Rembrandt-like gloom."

Despite her lack of formal education, Amelia Opie was intelligent enough to perceive woman's role in society. While resembling some of her sister writers in not fully participating in this subordinate role herself, she certainly advocated pious, submissive, and domestic behavior for other women. She did this by constructing her plots from the lives of less-fortunate people, women whom she had observed or read about. One of her adventures took her to an assize court, and she went back several times to listen to the pathetic cases tried there. Consequently, some of the characters in her novels are based on those who figured in these court sessions.

Her first novel, *Father and Daughter*, published in 1801, is about a young woman named Agnes Fitzhenry, whom the narrator calls a "helpless victim of passion [who]. . .yielded to the persuasions of a villain, and set off with him to Scotland." The rest of Agnes's life is, to the time of her early death, a series of misfortunes. Hannah More could not have been more mistaken when she claimed that somehow the fallen women in this novel are presented in a most exhilarating light.

It took only one wrong move for a nineteenth-century middle-class woman to be morally destroyed, and this appears to be Amelia Opie's message. Initially, Agnes conforms to the classic stereotype of a lower-middle-class girl. She is a beautiful, pious, dutiful daughter, the apple of her father's eye, until she naively falls in love with Clifford, an officer in the guards. She goes off with him, supposedly to get married, but he repeatedly deceives her by offering flimsy excuses for postponing the wedding. Agnes, who has been brought up like most lower-middle-class girls, totally sheltered from the world, and unprepared for such ugly realities, never suspects that her lover is dishonest.

She discovers that she is pregnant while Clifford is away. The narrator offers some didactic propaganda to warn young girls of the trials of childbearing in general, and of childbearing out of wedlock in particular. "The time of Agnes' confinement now drew near, a time which fills with apprehension even the wife who is soothed and supported by the tender attentions of an anxious husband, and the assiduities of affectionate relations and friends, and who know the child she is about to present them with, will at once gratify their affections and their pride; what then must have been the sensations of Agnes at a moment so awful and so dangerous as this." In those times, women, with or without husbands, were dying in childbirth every day.

When her child is six months old, Agnes finally learns that she is only one of many women whom Clifford has seduced. He is, in fact, to be married to an heiress. "Is it for a wretch like [Clifford]. . .[that] I have forsaken the best of parents," Agnes exclaims, as she begins her dramatic journey along the road to repentance.

She discovers that her father is an inmate at Bedlam, "driven mad by his daughter's desertion and disgrace." He no longer recognizes Agnes, the implication being that once a woman commits a moral offense against society, she becomes an outcast. Presumably her original goodness has been obliterated to the point where she is morally, spiritually, and physically, unrecognizable.

Agnes dedicates her life to caring for her father and, she hopes, restoring him to sanity. The old man finally recognizes his daughter—on his deathbed—and both the fallen daughter and the heartbroken father, who die within minutes of each other, are "borne to the same grave."

By means of a letter that Agnes receives from her childhood friend, Caroline Seymour, who is now happily married, Opie further expresses her sentiments on so-called fallen women. Caroline writes: "In my opinion, mistaken writers of both sexes, have endeavoured to prove that many an amiable woman has been for ever lost to virtue and the world, and become the victim of prostitution, merely because her first fault was treated with ill-judging and criminal severity. She moralistically adds that this "is calculated to deter the victim of seduction from penitence and amendment."

This statement is unintentionally ironic, for Agnes, although she has a child out of wedlock, is never promiscuous, and she is repentant. It is society that denies her the opportunity to live as a decent human being. And Opie, society's spokeswoman, gives Agnes no chance to expiate her "crime" and resume a normal life.

As this example shows, early-nineteenth-century women were given few choices either by society or by its representatives, women writers. In *Susan Gray*, a "little book" designed for working-class Sunday-school girls and written in 1802 by Mary Martha Butt Sherwood, the heroine is innocent. It is the people with whom she comes into contact who are responsible for her questionable reputation. As Sherwood demonstrates, notoriety, deserved or not, is virtually impossible to eradicate once established.

Susan Gray is the working-class sister of Agnes Fitzhenry. The narrator, a clergyman, never doubted that Susan, beautiful, pious, and with doting parents — her mother was "a most kind and dutiful wife" — "would become a good Christian." When Susan is six, however, both her parents die. On her own deathbed at the age of nineteen, she appears, through no fault of her own, as a fallen woman. It is at this point that the narrator meets her. Before Susan expires, she tells him that she has suffered "many trials and temptations," but that she is now "above the power of wicked pleasures" and has no desire "to be restored to health and return again to the busy and wicked world." She then relates her story. Her sixth to thirteenth years were spent with a wicked aunt who drank, swore, and beat her. When the aunt dies, Susan goes to live with a pious, old, rich lady, Mrs. Neale, who sends Susan to a day school and gives her clothes and, above all, a Bible. Like the Morrison girls of Glenburnie, Susan adopts the life-style of a proper lower-class girl. She learns to read her catechism and to do needlework and housework. Dutifully fulfilling her role as pious servant, Susan explains that these were "the happiest years of. . .[her] life." Before Mrs. Neale dies, she tells Susan that she has arranged for her to live with a woman, Mrs. Bennet, whom Susan will assist in washing, ironing, and sewing so that, after three years, Susan will "be fit to wait upon a lady."

While Mrs. Bennet, who is obviously intimidated by Mrs. Neale's social position, impresses the latter as being a good and honest woman, she is in reality crude and cruel. Mrs. Bennet and her friend, Charlotte, lack all of the "cardinal virtues" of womanhood. They do not read the Scriptures, nor do they attend church. They spend their time gossiping about "idle and unprofitable things," and they eventually conspire to ruin Susan's reputation. A handsome captain — a rake like Clifford, the officer who ruined Agnes in *Father and Daughter* — comes to town. Mrs. Bennet and Charlotte send him to their cottage to seduce Susan.

The captain flatters Susan and lies to her — promising marriage if she will consent to go away with him. But Susan refuses to see him. Although she remains locked in her attic room, the neighbors see him coming and going every night. Mrs. Bennet orders poor Susan to leave — without giving her a work reference. Beset by these circumstances, Susan has to choose between two evils: to go off with the captain in dishonor; or face dishonor and starvation at home. She dramatically escapes from Mrs. Bennet's cottage through a bedroom window and is caught in a ferocious storm. Consequently, she becomes severely ill, and after she has told her story, she dies.

Susan, the clergyman-narrator explains, gladly embraces death. "Never," he says, "did anyone prepare for death with so much joy, such holy hope and humble confidences in God." Actually, except for such platitudinous statements, *Susan Gray* fails as an argument for morality, for Susan is never given a choice. In *The Cottagers of Glenburnie*, the McClarty girls fall of their own volition, and in *Father and Daughter* Agnes allows Clifford to seduce her. Susan Gray, however, was a victim of the malice of others. The novel is one of the saddest commentaries on the plight of the early-nineteenth-century woman. Denied all choice, Susan's one salvation is to embrace death. Her only hope is to find the peace and honor in death that she was unable to find in life.

Not only does the innocent Susan Gray suffer unjustly, but, characteristically, the evil women of the novel suffer infinitely more than the evil man. Mrs. Bennet ends up miserably in the poorhouse, where she suffers for five years before she dies; Charlotte, after living with the captain in London for a month, is cast out by him when his rich wife returns. After seven wicked and wretched years, she too dies miserably, in a garret. But the captain, after deceiving and ruining two working girls, and, in all probability, scores of others, dies totally unrepentant "shortly after" leaving Charlotte.

Despite the unhappy lives of the characters in this novel, *Susan Gray* achieved great popularity. In her memoirs Mary Martha Butt Sherwood explains that *Susan Gray* "was, in its time, so great a favorite, that it was pirated in every shape and form, and. . .it would be impossible to calculate the editions through which it passed before the year 1816, when the copyright was returned to. . .[her]." And she adds: "In that year. . .[I] altered and sold it again." This dichotomy between the elevated purpose and the sordid content of the exemplary novels has been termed the "paradox of fiction" by Lionel Stevenson in *The English Novel: A Panorama*. "The popular novels," he writes about the works of this period, "were full of smug and pompous moral preachments, but the plots centered upon cruelty and lust and other evil passions."[1] Characters such as the evil captain, Mrs. Bennet, and Charlotte in *Susan Gray*, Clifford in *Father and Daughter*, and later Lord Howard in *The Divorced* were supposed to frighten the readers into good behavior.

As in fiction, life for lower-middle-class and lower-class women could be totally wretched because of a simple mistake; for upper-middle-class and upper-class women who attempted to redefine their role in society there was little satisfaction. The one difference between them and their lower-class sisters was material. Neither Adeline Mowbray in Amelia Opie's *Mother and Daughter* nor Lady Howard in Charlotte Bury's *The Divorced* are in want of food, clothing, servants, and shelter, but as payment for their defiance of society's rules, they face the same ostracism and emotional turmoil as their poor counterparts.

Since the most important event in an early-nineteenth-century woman's life was marriage, it is no coincidence that the problems that arise in *Mother and Daughter* and in *The Divorced* are marital. Adeline rejects the legal and religious bases of marriage. Rather, she believes that a marital relation-ship should be spiritual, intellectual, emotional, and perma-nent. In *The Divorced* Lady Howard's situation is similar in that she, too, is looking for a true love relationship, albeit legal. When she fails to find it with her first husband, she decides to divorce him in order to marry a man she feels that she truly loves. Today such aspirations in women would be judged perfectly acceptable; however, in early-nineteenth-century England, divorce and cohabitation outside of marriage were condemned.

"Education," however scanty, was often blamed for a young woman's errors. Just as Elizabeth Inchbald blamed Miss Milner's irresponsibility on her improper education, so Amelia Opie blamed Adeline Mowbray's shortcomings on her mother's lackadaisical methods: "After having overnight arranged the tasks of Adeline for the next day. . .[Mrs. Mowbray] would lie in bed all the morning, exposing that child to the dangers of idleness." Idleness was thought by the more moralistic members of society to breed discontent, so obviously Adeline was bound to end up searching for new ideas and life-styles.

In *Mother and Daughter* Opie criticizes the upper-middle-class blue stocking, rather than the immoral lower-middle-class woman of *Father and Daughter*. Mrs Mowbray is an in-tellectual of sorts, and intellectualism in women was frowned upon. "She would always insist on making the gentlemen of her acquaintance. . .engage with her in some literary or political conversation. She wanted to convert every drawing-room into an arena for the mind, and all her guests into intellectual gladiators." Even with her intellectual pretensions, however, when Mrs. Mowbray becomes a widow, she capitulates to society and remarries, despite the fact that her new husband, Sir Patrick, is interested only in her money and admits to "a criminal passion" for her daughter, Adeline.

In the face of this hypocrisy, Adeline decides to live with her lover, Glenmurray, in a union, she says that is, "Founded on rational grounds and cemented by rational ties." Despite her lover's protestations that "no wife was ever more pure than [she]," Glenmurray's friends, one by one, snub Adeline. When she becomes pregnant, Adeline briefly considers marriage, but only for the sake of her child. When she miscarries, she again decides against the legal ceremony.

Society, however, proves a formidable foe, and Adeline's situation worsens progressively. First, her mother becomes estranged from her because of her "immorality." Next, Glenmurray loses most of his money and becomes ill. On his deathbed he begs Adeline — he says it is his "dying request" — to marry his best friend, Berrendale, who is in love with her. He explains that her "only chance for happiness is [in] becoming a wife." "Few men," he adds, "will be likely to marry you after your connection with me."

At first the strong-willed Adeline protests, but she eventually marries Berrendale, who subsequently neglects and mistreats her. But Adeline, like Lady Howard in *The Divorced*, welcomes the cruel treatment. "She fancies that all the sufferings she underwent were trials which she was doomed to undergo, as punishments for the crime she had committed in leaving her mother and living with Glenmurray."

Shortly after the Berrendales have a child, Adeline learns that her husband has been having an affair with a servant. The double standard is quite apparent, for the only repercussion is that Berrendale, out of guilt, becomes more attentive to Adeline.

But his attentiveness does not last, and he soon leaves for Jamaica. Adeline, since she has no friends, is lonelier than ever. Berrendale dies shortly after, but not before Adeline learns that he had planned to marry a wealthy woman. Adeline, quite ill, is finally reunited with her mother, to whom she admits that she has "experienced the anguish of being forsaken, despised, and disgraced in the eyes of the world." Her final desire is that her mother raise her daughter and "teach her no opinions that can destroy her sympathies with general society, and make her an alien to the hearts of those amongst whom she lives."

Although Amelia Opie dramatizes many of her own ideas, the basic story of Adeline Mowbray is derived from the life of Mary Wollstonecraft. As one of Opie's biographers explains, "both [Adeline and Mary] tried to be philosophers, both tried to consider the mere ceremony of marriage as useless and unnecessary, and both had reason bitterly to rue their mistake." A heroine who deviated from society's norm was doomed.

Critics who condescended to review the work praised both its subject and the lesson it taught. "These volumes," said the critic for the *Monthly Review, or Literary Journal*, "are. . .so superior to those which we usually encounter under the title of novels [presumably those novels which glorify defiance of social mores] that we can safely recommend them to the perusal of our readers."[2]

Lady Howard, the central figure in Charlotte Bury's *The Divorced*, also has reason to bitterly rue her mistake. This didactic work describes the consequences that a divorced woman faced in England in the first half of the nineteenth century. The picture is so grim that one reviewer, while acknowledging that "the consequences of crime are misery," criticized the novel for depicting "unconditional misery from first to last." He further explained that the "end of imaginative literature. . .is to excite pleasurable feelings."[3] Nevertheless, gloomy works such as *The Divorced*, *Susan Gray*, and *Father and Daughter* were extremely popular among women readers. This vicarious, albeit often harrowing, participation offered a relief from their dull, routine lives.

The Divorced begins with a flashback in which Lady Alice, the daughter of Lord and Lady Howard, is rejected by her dearest playmate, Fanny Harcourt, whose mother forbids her to associate with the daughter of a divorced woman. The reader then learns that sixteen years previously Lady Howard, bored with her first husband, Lord Vernon, left him and their son (by law, the husband got custody of the child) in order to marry Lord Howard, her husband's friend. While Lady Howard had "sacrificed everything — rank, station, consideration, virtue" — to marry the man she loved, her husband, Lord Howard, refers to her as "an albatross," and makes sure that she is the butt of "rebukes, reproaches, and angry allegations." Her "mistake" — not his — is repeatedly referred to as a "crime," for, as the narrator explains, "The world [has] decided the question of wrong and right, as to make the man. . . immaculate, the woman impure; though the one is thrust out of society, the latter is courted and well received." Similarly, Lady Howard tells her husband after he insults her: "You charge me with a crime of which you were the author, and in which you share, although the customs of society exonerate the man from all penalty in our case and place it solely on the woman." Nevertheless, Lady Howard accepts the standards of the world. She views herself as a sinner and, like Adeline Mowbray and Agnes Fitzhenry, recognizes the social realities of deviant behavior. When her son by Lord Howard, Lord Talbot, asks her what became of Lady Vernon (Talbot is friendly with Lord Stuart Vernon without realizing that he is his half-brother), Lady Howard answers: "She is not dead, but worse." Similarly, when Fanny Harcourt explains the divorce, she calls it a "sad consequence. . .[arising] out of the light conduct of our sex."

Charlotte Bury
(Present location unknown.)
COURTESY OF THE NATIONAL PORTRAIT GALLERY, LONDON

Charlotte Bury's presentation of woman as the weaker sex is revealed not only in the "light conduct" of Lady Howard, but also in the description of Lady Alice, the Howards' daughter, and in the effect that Alice has on others. Lord Howard comments on his daughter: "Alice's unquestioned regularity of form and feature, the suffrages of artists." He realizes that "the unbounded and general admiration of men will excite envy in the greater portion of her own sex; and it must be confessed that it is upon the latter that much of a woman's peace depends." Again we see the woman — a jealous woman in this case — as her own worst enemy.

The courtship of Alice and her beau, the young Lord Leicester, is traditional and completely in accord with society's values. Lady Alice exhibits her drawings and prints; Leicester carries the conversation. If their courtship is traditional, however, Alice's parentage is not. When Lady Margaret, Leicester's mother, finds out about the relationship, she is aghast and exclaims: "The blood of the Leicesters is to be defiled; their honours sullied by an alliance, not of inferior birth — for I could have borne that misfortune — but to think of the pollution of vice, the degradation of being allied to a family who are branded with crime — horrible," and she forbids the marriage.

Lord Talbot returns home with tuberculosis, and Lady Alice is occupied nursing her brother until his death, for which Lord Howard cruelly blames his wife. Colonel Leicester goes to Greece to fight and travel — men could apparently forget by physically escaping from their troubles — but Lady Alice stays home, pining for her lover; then she contracts tuberculosis and dies.

Thus, the characterization of the two females in *The Divorced* is stereotypic. Both Lady Howard and her daughter, Lady Alice, are weak and subordinate. The portrayal of Lord Howard as a cruel, often tyrannical, man is equally one-dimensional. It is implied, however, that society, or more specifically, his wife's crime against society, has turned him into a tyrant. Lord Howard's attitude toward women, divorced or otherwise, is contemptuous and, evidently, not unusual for the period. When Lady Howard attempts to defend herself from his rebukes, he replies: "Well, madam, that is not a bad oration. I supposed you practised public speaking: d — —d provoking to have an educated wife! No woman ought to learn to read or write. More harm comes of stuffing their weak brains with matters too high for them, than any advantage that ever was gained by it." Earlier, Lord Howard blames his wife for their situation when he rationalizes that "women are always so full of contrivances, so wise in their own conceits — so foolish in the great conduct of human life."

Eventually, both Lord Vernon and Lord Howard die, but Lady Howard lives, ostracized and friendless, to suffer for the remainder of her life. Charlotte Bury echoes her contemporary Maria Edgeworth in suggesting man's weakness and woman's strength. Lord Howard shoots himself, but Lady Howard, whose trial is much worse, never contemplates suicide, the coward's way out.

Instead, she lives frugally on money from the sale of her jewelry and spends the last years of her life with her first son, Lord Stuart Vernon, and his wife. When she dies, her son does not bury her next to the graves of her husband and children, but among strangers. Although he has befriended his mother, he has not forgiven her. In a society that condemns rationality and cultivates hypocrisy, one could hardly expect a divorcée to be forgiven — even by her son. (At a dinner that Lord Howard attends before his death, for example, he overhears the following conversation in praise of adultery: "Mrs.—— is a very wise woman. In her present position she has all the advantages and none of the disadvantages which she would have had if she became his wife. She has escaped the disgrace of being a divorcée. I am always surprised when a woman sacrifices her position by running off. It is so easy to manage the affair skillfully, and not to pay too high a price for it.")

Charlotte Bury concludes her novel with this moral: "Lady Howard's history affords a fearful example to those whose affections, like hers, are unhallowed — to those who stand at the brink of the precipice. Oh! may all such take warning from this melancholy statement." Bury's novel, however, is more of a warning to women than a criticism of society. Women authors seemed to be as afraid of society as were the characters that they portrayed.

Not all women writers, however, concentrated their major efforts on warning women of the sad consequences of departing from society's mores or on dramatizing how women could gain happiness by submission to a social stereotype. Women writers, in the Gothic novel, proved that they were able to present women in situations that were more improbable, romantic, and exciting than the real situations in their everyday lives — without changing the stereotypic female characters. Even so exceptional a woman as Mary Shelley, who alone among women novelists was capable of producing an intellectual novel, did not escape from the stereotype of woman as unintellectual and largely passive.

Because of the vicarious pleasure that the Gothic novelist provided, their works were much in demand. This explanation is suggested in Mary Wollstonecraft's novel, *Wrongs of Women* (1793), in which one of the female characters, who is ashamed of her emotional outburts over trifling situations, realizes how hard it is for women with no active duties or pursuits to avoid being romantic.

The first Gothic novel, *The Castle of Otranto*, was written by Horace Walpole in 1764. Women writers, emulating Wollstonecraft's female character, were intrigued by this form. One woman, Clara Reeve (1729-1807), sought to improve on Walpole's method. Her five novels, the most famous of which is *The Champion of Virtue, a Gothic Story* (1777), reissued and retitled a year later as *The Old English Baron*, employ a similar setting to Walpole's and the "same central plot motif," but provide "a rational explanation for each apparently supernatural event."[4] Another woman, Charlotte Smith (1749-1806), wrote several novels of Gothic terror in rapid succession. She was known especially for her heroines, who were often glorified after extensive suffering, and for her creative use of scenery "to enhance the moods of her characters."[5]

Ann Radcliffe (1764-1823), who was to become the best-known Gothic novelist, utilized Clara Reeve's rational explanations in her novels, as well as Charlotte Smith's atmospheric descriptions. The romantic ideas for her novels came both from her readings and from her imagination. She did not involve herself in literary society, or, for that matter, in society at all. Her husband was the editor and owner of a weekly paper, the *English Chronicle*, which he worked on nightly. Since she had no children, Ann Radcliffe began to write. Still, she did not wish to be considered an author. It was said that "a mystery hangs over her almost as great as that of her own Udolpho."[6] While Radcliffe was still alive, a report circulated that she had died mad—a madness, it was said, that was the effect of her powerful imagination. Subsequently, a clergyman composed an *Ode to Terror* to commemorate the event. Radcliffe, who lived another thirteen years, never bothered to contradict the report.

Ann Radcliffe did not seem to care whether the world thought her to be dead or alive, but she did, like her predecessor Clara Reeve, care a great deal about reality in her horror tales. One of the major criticisms of her novels was that she had an unfortunate fancy for explaining away her horrors at the end of her books, which always ruined the effect. Apparently she could never quite accept the idea of pure supernaturalism. The mysterious noises that Emily St. Aubert, the protagonist in *The Mysteries of Udolpho*, hears in the chateau are caused by outlaws trying to frighten away the owners.

Not only is there a rational explanation for the events in the novel, but there is also an explanation for the female characters. Although Radcliffe does not explicitly state it, all of the heroines in her Gothic novels implicitly conform to society's stereotype. In an early description of Radcliffe's heroine, Emily St. Aubert, in *The Mysteries of Udolpho*, the narrator states that "she had discovered in her early years uncommon delicacy of mind, warm affections, and ready benevolence; but with these was observable a ready degree of susceptibility too exquisite to admit of lasting peace." What the narrator seems to be suggesting is that Emily feels emotions too keenly, that her sensibility is excessive. This was a natural feminine inclination according to late-eighteenth-century authorities on women, but as Mary Wollstonecraft later pointed out in *Vindication*, and as Ann Radcliffe seemed to realize, woman is perfectly capable of resisting such emotionalism. Despite her sensiblity, Emily does maintain self-discipline.

When her father dies shortly after her mother's death, Emily is left with an unfeeling aunt. The aunt marries Signor Montoni, a sinister Italian who prevents Emily from marrying Valencourt, her lover, and who forces both Emily and her aunt to live in his castle, Udolpho. He mistreats his wife because she will not sign over her land to him; she eventually dies, leaving the property to Emily. Montoni, after subjecting Emily to many harrowing experiences, forces her to sign over the estate. Finally, Emily escapes, the authorities force Montoni to return her property, and she marries Valencourt.

Emily exercises her self-discipline in a threatening interchange between Signor Montoni and herself. As one recent critic suggests, Emily and Montoni represent the "pure, pale maiden persecuted by a vicious but dominating sadist [which] became a powerful sex symbol for both male and female readers."[7] Emily, despite her sensibility and emotionalism, does not succumb that easily. Although Montoni manages to wreak his revenge on his wife by causing her death—he locks her in a room for seven years—Emily proves more formidable. When she refuses to turn her land over to him, he is shocked by her audacity and says: "I have been mistaken in my opinion of you,. . .you speak boldly, and presumptuously, upon a subject which you do not understand. For once I am willing to pardon the conceit of ignorance; the weakness of your sex, from which, it seems you are not exempt." "But," he adds, "if you persist in this strain—you have everything to fear from my justice." Emily, however, is not afraid and answers: "The strength of my mind is equal to the justice of my cause." "You speak like a heroine, Montoni says, "We shall see whether you can suffer like one." Emily does, for she becomes involved in a series of unpleasant situations: her aunt's pitiful death, almost being kidnapped by nuns, and generally fearing for her life in Montoni's castle.

But even though she can match wits with her uncle, she is still a traditional heroine. She is pious, for she "frequently address[es] herself to Heaven for support and protection," and her "pious prayers," the narrator tells us, are "accepted. . .[by] God." She is domestic, since it is she who comforts her poor aunt during her last days and also prepares the body. She is pure, since she agrees to marry Valencourt, her lover, only after she is convinced that he is honest and righteous and therefore deserving of her hand.

The plots of all of Ann Radcliffe's novels—indeed, of all Gothic novels—were merely formulaic. As Joyce Marjorie Sanxter Tompkins summarizes it in her book on the novel, "A beautiful and solitary girl is persecuted in picturesque surroundings, and after many fluctuations of fortune, during which she seems again and again on the point of reaching safety, only to be thrust back into the midst of perils, is restored to her friends and marries the man of her choice."[8]

Ann Radcliffe's romances were "the rage" among many of her reviewers, as well as among her readers.[9] Catherine J. Hamilton summarizes Radcliffe's influence on three of the prominent writers of the early nineteenth century: "Hazlitt said that he owed his love of moonlit night, autumn leaves, and decaying ruins to her influence, Byron condescended to imitate her [in *Manfred*, for example], and Walter Scott was among her warmest admirers."[10] *The Monk* (1795), by Matthew Lewis, was begun during his stay in Germany and was finished under the influence of *The Mysteries of Udolpho*.

Another popular Gothic novel was Mary Shelley's *Frankenstein*, written in 1818. In contrast to *Udolpho*, however, *Frankenstein* is one of the few novels by a woman in which the women characters, accurately reflecting their position in society, are of secondary importance. This is perhaps because *Frankenstein* is more than a Gothic tale. It is philosophical as well, suggesting the modern idea that man's innate good is perverted by society—Frankenstein abandons his creation—and an example of psychological realism, for a man is rejected on the basis of appearance alone. In the intellectual novel of that time, the main character would naturally be male. Reviewers who praised the writing, even though they felt that the subject matter was rather macabre, assumed that the author of *Frankenstein*, which was originally published anonymously, was a man. *Blackwood's Edinburgh Magazine*, for instance, attributed the work to Percy Bysshe Shelley because of its similarity to Godwin's *St. Leon*. The work was favorably noticed by both *Blackwood's Edinburgh Magazine* and the *Quarterly Review*. The former praised the novel for its "original genius," its "plain and forcible English without exhibiting that mixture of hyperbolical Germanisms with which tales of wonder are usually told."[11] The latter, while contending that the author must be "as mad as his hero," asserted that "there is something tremendous in the unmeaning hollowness of its sound and the vague obscurity of its images."[12] The *Quarterly* reviewer, however, criticized *Frankenstein* on the grounds that "it inculcates no lessons of conduct, manners, or morality."[13] He lost sight of the fact that *Frankenstein* is a philosophical novel with a masculine protagonist, and not an exemplary, manneristic work with a female heroine.

Victor Frankenstein, the central character, is a young scientist who creates, with help from "the dissecting room and the

Mary Shelley
COURTESY OF THE NATIONAL PORTRAIT GALLERY, LONDON

slaughterhouse," a hideous monster. He assumes no respon- sibility for his creation (indeed, his attitude is monstrous), and, consequently, the monster turns on him and attempts to destroy all those to whom Frankenstein is close. The story is farfetched and brings to mind a comment that Maria Edgeworth made to her father when he reacted to the novel *O'Donnél* by Sydney Owenson Morgan. "This is quite im- probable," he said, and Maria retorted: "Never mind the im- probability, let us go on with the entertainment."[14] And *Frankenstein* is entertaining, though bizarre, for Mary Shelley, daughter of two fine writers, Mary Wollstonecraft and William Godwin, and wife of the poet Percy Bysshe Shelley, was an ex- tremely talented young woman. She was only nineteen when she wrote the novel as a game of sorts, a contest on a stormy night among Shelley, Lord Byron, Claire Claremont (Mary's half sister), Dr. John Polidori, and Mary, to see who could pro- duce the best Gothic tale.

Although Mary was able to write a cleverer tale than the talented men in her company, the women in her novel are strictly passive. There are four women in *Frankenstein*, each of whom is a helpless waif rescued by a man. There is Victor Frankenstein's mother, Caroline, who supported her father "selflessly" by "plaiting straw" and other "plain work." When her father dies, leaving her an orphan and a beggar, Caroline is placed in the care of a relative by Mr. Frankenstein, who marries her two years later. Mr. Frankenstein and his wife then adopt Elizabeth, a beautiful girl whose poor parents cannot af- ford to keep her, who becomes betrothed to Victor Franken- stein, the hero. Elizabeth is described in Platonic im- agery—recalling the Renaissance poets' stereotypic descrip- tions of women. "Her hair was the brightest living gold, and. . . seemed to set a crown of distinction on her head. Her brow was clean and ample, her blue eyes cloudless, and her lips and the moulding of her face so expressive of sensibility and sweetness, that none could behold her without looking on her as a distinct species, a being heaven-sent, and bearing a celestial stamp in all her features."

The Frankensteins also care for Justine, a poor girl who becomes their servant. The monster resides near a large farm-house where he observes another girl, Safie, who is cared for by the father of her betrothed before her marriage. Nearly all of these women are, or will serve as, helpmates or companions of men. This is precisely what Frankenstein's monster desires — a female monster in whom he will "excite sympathy" and who will fulfill his "dreams of bliss."

Although a woman could write an original and multidimensional novel in the early nineteenth century, she could still present only one-dimensional, stereotyped women characters.

Lionel Stevenson offers an explanation for the ineffectual characterizations in many of the novels of the late eighteenth and early nineteenth centuries. "In the Gothic novels," he says, "the characters were puppets, adopting attitudes of terror or nobility; in the novels of doctrine they were specimens of social tendencies or mouthpieces for the authors' [or society's] opinions."[15] If the characters' minds were not stimulating, their lives were dramatic, and the influence that they had on their largely feminine audience was profound. It was a man's world, and the women novelists of the period, although talented, knowledgeable, and versatile, did little or nothing to change it. The lives of women, even of many women writers, were, for the most part, stifling and dull. Most women, for better or worse, would rather have been heroines.

NOTES

1. Lionel Stevenson, *The English Novel: A Panorama* (Boston: Houghton Mifflin Co., 1960), p. 176.

2. *Monthly Review or Literary Journal* 51 (1806): 320.

3. *Athenaeum* (1837), p. 135.

4. Stevenson, *The English Novel*, p. 151.

5. Ibid., p. 162.

6. Catherine J. Hamilton, *Women Writers: Their Works and Ways*, 1st ser. (1892; reprint ed., New York: Books for Libraries Press, 1971), p. 146.

7. Stevenson, *The English Novel*, p. 165.

8024

8. Joyce Marjorie Sanxter Tompkins, *The Popular Novel in England, 1770-1800* (London: Constable & Co., 1932).

9. Hamilton, *Women Writers*, p. 144.

10. Ibid.

11. *Blackwood's Edinburgh Magazine* 2, no. 12 (March 1818): 619.

12. *Quarterly Review* 28, no. 36 (January 1818): 385.

13. Ibid.

14. Lionel Stevenson, *The Wild Irish Girl: The Life of Sydney Owenson, Lady Morgan, 1776-1859* (London: Chapman & Hall, 1936), p. 167.

15. Stevenson, *The English Novel*, p. 173.

7
Writers against Rights:
The Feminine Irony

The woman who is known only through a man is known wrong.[1]

— Mary Beard

Early-nineteenth-century writers subscribed to, internalized, and projected society's views of women in their writing. Despite the French Revolution's demand for liberty, equality, and fraternity, English society, perpetuating tradition, continued to view women as second-class citizens. There were essentially two categories: women of the middle and upper classes and women of the lower, or working, class. Working-class women often had more equality, for the economic expansion resulting from the Industrial Revolution made it possible for them to work for wages in factories, in shops, on farms, and even in coal mines. These women were also freed from their homes; in the labor fields, they not only competed against men but earned their own money.

Still, women were discriminated against in terms of wages and job security. Men were the breadwinners; women were merely helpers or apprentices. Between running their homes, bearing children, and holding a job, working-class women received little if any education; most were illiterate. In a rigidly entrenched class system, even though the education of working-class men was limited, they were usually taught to read and write. While young boys attended school, their sisters were at home caring for the younger children, in addition to cooking and cleaning. Their mothers, meanwhile, were working in factories or on farms.

Although the working woman toiled long hours for meager pay, she probably felt a sense of accomplishment, or, at least, of performing a necessary role. Marriage was not necessarily her only goal, as it was for her idle, dependent middle-class sisters. If she were single, she could earn enough to support herself. If she were single with children, she could always count on the parish to support her and her family, and on the moral laxity prevalent in the mills and mines that allowed her to continue working. Good workers, including unmarried mothers, were in great demand.

While the working-class woman was using her ability in the labor market to raise the life-style of the middle and upper classes, it was the middle- and upper-class woman who was respected — and respected essentially for her lack of ability. Society in general and, specifically, her father and later her husband, in what seems a rationalization of her inferior status, placed her on a pedestal, treated her like a goddess, and prevented her from participating in any serious pursuit in the mainstream of English life. Marriage was the only option available to the middle- and upper-class woman; her entire upbringing was geared to this end. Even among such enlightened and liberal critics as Dr. John Gregory, marriage as a goal was stressed. In *A Father's Legacy to his Daughters*, Gregory writes that, on the one hand, he knows "nothing that renders a woman more despicable, than her thinking it essential to happiness to be married." On the other, he continues: "I am of the opinion that. . .[a woman] may attain a superior degree of happiness in a married state, to what. . .[she] can possibly find in any other." He explains: "I know the forlorn and unprotected situation of an old maid, the chagrin and peevishness which are apt to infect their tempers."[2]

Similarly, Jane West in *The Advantages of Education* describes a mother telling her daughter: "If you aspire to the honour of his hand, I would advise you in some degree to give up your books and your garden and apply yourself to the sciences of the card table and the toilet."

In nineteenth-century society a woman's life began with her marriage. At least she was considered as being secure and respectable, and as fulfilling the expectations of her parents and her friends—indeed, of the whole society. Ironically, a woman's life also ended with marriage. Men had their professions, as well as their diversions and entertainment; they could frequent private clubs or ale houses, depending upon their station in life. But women were relegated to the home. Some women left the house only to go to church, although among the lower middle classes, some wives and maidservants might go to market in order to sell poultry, eggs, or other produce. Among the upper classes, women might go by carriage to have afternoon tea with a friend or to a musical with a lover—discreetly.

As was stated earlier, "piety," "purity," "submissiveness," and "domesticity" were the four "cardinal virtues"—qualities that suggest a seraph rather than a woman. Woman was revered, humored, sheltered, and fussed over, but never treated as an equal.

Bored and repressed, she became a devotee of both fiction and nonfiction by men and especially by women writers, who internalized society's attitudes toward women and dramatized them in their writings. There were perhaps three reasons why women writers perpetuated women's subordinate position. The first was practical diplomacy. Hannah More and Maria Edgeworth, for instance, two of the more prolific and famous women writers of the period, were well aware of the emphasis on "cardinal virtues," or of society's expectations, for women. And both attempted to reach a vast audience. Maria

Edgeworth wrote fiction for children as well as adults. Hannah More's nonfiction included works on education, religion, and morals; her imaginative works consisted of plays and novels. She also wrote political ballads. In addition, she geared her writing to the various social classes. Other women writers, while unable to participate in lawmaking, were, nevertheless, political.

They were also rebelling in a hypocritical sort of way—for they were not practicing what they preached. Hannah More, Maria Edgeworth, Elizabeth Hamilton, Mary Russell Mitford, and many other women writers of the late eighteenth and early nineteenth centuries were unmarried and better educated than the women for whom they wrote. None, however, was as perfect as her heroines. The feminine stereotype, too perfect to exist in reality, yet created by women—women writers—is satirized by Lord Byron in *Don Juan:*

> In short, she was a walking calculation,
>   Miss Edgeworth's novels stepping from
>   their covers,
> Or Mrs. Trimmer's books on education,
>   Or 'Coelebs' wife' set out in quest of
>   lovers,
> Morality's prim personification
>   In which not Envy's self a flaw discovers;
> To others' share let 'female errors fall,'
> For she had not even one—the worst of all.
>   (Canto 1, line 16)

The third reason that women writers presented women as they did was perhaps naiveté. Writers such as Mary Martha Butt Sherwood, Jane West, and Ann Taylor reflected rather than questioned society's values. Their works were mainly didactic: as writers they would guide women in performing their proper roles as subordinate creatures, as helpmates to men. In attempting to be messiahs to women, they often ended up as the devil's disciples.

So long as women were willing to subscribe to the subordinate role created by society and endorsed by most women writers, their lives could not really change. As H. N. Brailsford describes Mary Wollstonecraft's point in *Vindication*, "Everything in the future of women depends on the revision of the attitude [not only] of men towards women. . .[but also] of women towards themselves."[3] As long as women writers sought to educate women to be contented with their lot, to stay in their place, as did Elizabeth Hamilton in *The Cottagers of Glenburnie*, where the narrator urges servant girls not to put on airs, or as in *Strictures*, where Hannah More decided that women should play four roles—those of "daughter, wife, mother, and mistress of her family"—women had virtually no chance of achieving any sort of independence or equality.

Nonfictional books by women consisted largely of manuals of prescribed behavior for females. Under the guise of treatises, religious works, and education texts, these books were merely guides on how to win husbands and, in marriage, how to live dutiful, pious lives. As might be expected, they ranged from the absurd to the sublime. Subjects ran the gamut from the marriage propaganda of Jane West, who deemed marriage a "heaven-ordained bond," to Ann Taylor's and Mary Wollstonecraft's sensible advice on the rearing of children. One of the most disturbing aspects of most of these nonfictional works is that, while the authors sometimes offer women sound philosophies by which to live, they fail to see that unless women become independent and equal they can never fully activate these philosophies. Hannah More suggests, for instance, that women have the kind of education that "inculcates principles, polishes taste. . .cultivates reason. . .habituates the reflection," but such a comprehensive education was simply not available to women. Even if women had been able to secure such an education, the question arises as to what they would have done with it.

Another of Hannah More's unrealistic pieces of advice to women is "to raise the depressed tone of public morals, and to awaken the drowsy spirit of religious principles." But it is questionable whether women confined to domesticity, in a continuous round of pregnancy and childbearing, and with few outside contacts, could ever have "raise[d]. . .public morals."

And herein lies a further irony. Women like Hannah More and Maria Edgeworth, to cite but two distaff writers, had an opportunity "to awaken the drowsy spirit of religious principles," for they were single, better educated, well-to-do, and they had their own pulpits—their published writings. By urging women to get married, bear children, and remain subservient, they simply projected society's views. They did not change women's position.

Other women novelists were no different. They presented women's lives as they—and as society—felt that they should be. The novels of manners, such as *Evelina*, *A Simple Story*, and *Marriage*, while interesting in their treatments of middle- and upper-class English society, nevertheless focused on the process of a young girl's "education" and socialization and concluded with marriage—the ultimate reward. Novels such as *The Cottagers of Glenburnie* and *Our Village*, depicting domestic life, urged women to accept their domestic role, their pious passivity, and, lest their readers be unconvinced, they dramatized the unhappy lives of repentant but hopeless sinners like Agnes Fitzhenry and Lady Howard, who were foolish enough to depart from the acceptable feminine pattern.

Although novels of manners and those dealing with the trials of domestic life attracted the largest number of female authors, women were also writing Gothic and historical novels. Although they treated the "ideal" female, they went a step further and expanded the reader's horizons. Nature, science, history, and genealogy went into the making of novels such as *Frankenstein* and *The Mysteries of Udolpho*. Although they were often better written and more enlightening, in keeping with the conventions of society, the central characters were usually men. Men in nineteenth-century English society could lead exciting and fulfilling lives in reality as well as in novels, but most English women of that period could hope to experience—vicariously—such excitement and fulfillment only through fiction.

While women authors wrote, often without knowing it, to reinforce women's subordinate position in life, they did provide some insight and a great deal of entertainment to idle and bored middle- and upper-class women. If their writings did not change the lives of their readers in particular or society as a whole, the mere fact that the authors were women, some of whom, like Fanny Burney, Maria Edgeworth, Mary Shelley, and Ann Radcliffe, were superior, did indicate that change was in the air. The change in the role of women writers from the first half of the nineteenth century, when women essentially wrote for and were read exclusively by women, to the Victorian period, when Mary Ann Evans and the Brontës were an integral part of the literary world and women in fiction became multidimensional, was more significant than the change in the role of women in general, who only in the late nineteenth and twentieth centuries began gaining their rights.

Although the writings of women did not significantly broaden the lives of their feminine readers, they certainly strengthened their own existences. When an anonymous critic, assuming that women poured their boredom and frustrations into their writings, stated that "happy women do not write," he could not have been farther from the truth. Of sixteen well-known nineteenth-century women writers discussed in Catherine J. Hamilton's *Women Writers: Their Works and Ways*, only one, Jane Austen, died before reaching the age of fifty. In a period when childbearing and diseases such as tuberculosis and typhus took an enormous toll and the average life span was much shorter than it is today, the excellent physical and mental health of these writers was striking. Seven of the sixteen lived to be over eighty, eleven lived to be over seventy, and twelve to be over sixty. Most of them, including Fanny Burney, Elizabeth Inchbald, Anna L. Barbauld, Hannah More, Ann Radcliffe, Maria Edgeworth, Amelia Opie, Susan

Ferrier, and Mary Russell Mitford, lived fulfilling, active lives. They undoubtedly shared the attitude toward life that the Scottish songstress Lady Anne Barnard, who lived to be seventy-five and was praised by Sir Walter Scott for her "pastoral" lyricism, expressed in her journal: "When alone, I am not above five-and-twenty, I can entertain myself with a succession of inventions which would be more effective if they were fewer. I forget that I am sixty-eight, and if by chance I see myself in the glass looking very abominable, I do not care. What is the moral of this? That as far as my experience goes (and it is said that we must be all physicians or fools at forty) occupation is the best nostrum in the great laboratory of human life for pains, cares, mortifications and ennui."

To paraphrase Mary Beard's contention that "the woman who is known only through a man is known wrong," the early-nineteenth-century woman who is known only through women writers is also known wrong. The average nineteenth-century woman lived an idle, useless, short life — often dying in childbirth — but the nineteenth-century woman writer was productive, imaginative, and useful; she also enjoyed comparative longevity. Her accomplishments in what was unquestionably a man's world were impressive, yet the final impact of what she wrote only reinforced the conceit of male domination — the ultimate feminine irony.

NOTES

1. Mary Beard, *Woman as a Force in History* (New York: Macmillan Co., 1946) p. 209.

2. Dr. John Gregory, *A Father's Legacy to His Daughters* (Boston: L. C. Bowles, 1822), p. 230.

3. Henry Noel Brailsford, *Shelley, Godwin, and Their Circle* (New York: Henry Holt & Co., 1913), p. 206.

Bibliography

Abbott, John S. C. *The Mother at Home; or, The Principles of Maternal Duty Familiarly Illustrated.* New York: Harper & Bros., 1852.

Acton, William. *Prostitution Considered in Its Moral, Social, and Sanitary Aspects.* 1857. Reprint. London: Frank Cass, 1972.

Adamson, J. W. *English Education, 1790-1902.* Cambridge: At the University Press, 1930.

Aries, Phillippe. *Centuries of Childhood: A Social History of Family Life.* New York: Vintage, 1962.

Armstrong, Martin. *Lady Hester Stanhope.* New York: Viking Press, 1928.

Athenaeum. London, 1837.

Baker, Eric W. *A Herald of the Evangelical Revival.* London: Epworth Press, 1948.

Baker, Ernest A. *A Guide to the Best Fiction in English.* New York: Macmillan Co., 1913.

——. *A History of the English Novel.* 11 vols. London: Witherby, 1924.

Baker, Ernest A., and Packman, James. *A Guide to the Best Fiction, English and American.* London: Routledge, 1932.

Banks, J. A., and Banks, Olive. *Feminism and Family Planning in Victorian England: Studies in the Life of Women.* New York: Schocken Books, 1964.

Barbauld, Anna Laetitia. *A Selection from the Poems and Prose Writings of Mrs. Anna Laetitia Barbauld.* Edited by Grace A. Ellis. Boston: Roberts Bros., 1874.

Barnett, George L., ed. *Eighteenth Century British Novelists on the Novel*. New York: Appleton-Century-Crofts, 1968.

Barry, Iris. *Portrait of Lady Mary Wortley Montagu*. New York: Bobbs-Merrill, 1928.

Beard, Mary. *Woman as a Force in History*. New York: Macmillan Co., 1946.

Blackwood's Edinburgh Magazine. London, 1817-19.

Brailsford, Henry Noel. *Shelley, Godwin, and Their Circle*. New York: Henry Holt & Co., 1913.

Briggs, Asa. *The Making of Modern England, 1783-1867: The Age of Improvement*. New York: Harper & Row, 1959.

Brinton, Crane; Christopher, John B.; and Wolff, Robert Lee. *Modern Civilization: A History of the Last Five Centuries*. 2d ed. Englewood Cliffs, N. J.: Prentice-Hall, 1967.

Broadhurst, Frances. "A Word in Favour of Female Schools: Addressed to Parents, Guardians, and the Public at Large." *Pamphleteer* 27 (1826): 453-73.

Broadhurst, Thomas. "Advice to Young Ladies on the Improvement of the Mind." 8 vols. London, 1808. Summarized and reviewed in *Edinburgh Review* 15 (1810): 299-315.

Burney, Fanny. *Evelina; or, The History of a Young Lady's Entrance into the World*, Edited by Edward A. Bloom. London: Oxford University Press, 1968.

Bury, Lady Charlotte. *The Divorced*. 1836. Reprint. Philadelphia: T. B. Peterson, 1836.

Cecil, Lord David. "Fanny Burney's Novels." *Essays on the Eighteenth Century Presented to D. Nichol Smith*. London: Oxford University Press, 1945.

Clark, G. Kitson. *The Making of Victorian England*. New York: Atheneum, 1972.

Clive, John. *Scotch Reviewers: The Edinburgh Review, 1802-1815*. Cambridge, Mass.: Harvard University Press, 1957.

Colby, Vineta. *The Singular Anomaly: Women Novelists of the Nineteenth Century*. New York: New York University Press, 1970.

————. *Yesterday's Woman: Domestic Realism in the English Novel*. Princeton, N.J.: Princeton University Press, 1974.

Critical Review. London, 1800-1814.

Cross, Wilbur. *The Development of the English Novel*. New York: Macmillan Co., 1900.

Cunnington, C. Willett. *Feminine Attitudes in the Nineteenth Century*. New York: Macmillan Co., 1936.

de Beauvoir, Simone. *The Second Sex*. Edited and translated by H. M. Parshley. New York: Modern Library, 1968.

Dobson, Austin. *Fanny Burney*. New York: Macmillan Co., 1903.

Doyle, Bryan, ed. and comp. *The Who's Who of Children's Literature*. 3d ed. New York: Schocken, 1971.

Edgeworth, Maria. *Belinda*. 1801. Reprint. New York: Macmillan Co., 1896.

———. *Castle Rackrent*. Edited by George Watson. 1800. Reprint. London: Macmillan & Co., 1964.

———. *The Parent's Assistant; or, Stories for Children*. New York: Harper & Bros., 1836.

———. *Practical Education*. 2 vols. New York: Self, Brown & Stansbury, 1801.

Edinburgh Review. London, 1802-24.

Ellmann, Mary. *Thinking About Women*. New York: Harcourt, Brace & World, 1968.

Elton, Oliver. *A Survey of English Literature, 1780-1830*. 2 vols. London: E. Arnold, 1924.

Ferrier, Susan. *Marriage, a Novel*. Edited by Herbert Foltinek. 1818. Reprint. London: Oxford University Press, 1971.

Flinn, M. W. *Origins of the Industrial Revolution*. London: Longmans, 1966.

Gentleman's Magazine. London, 1799-1824.

Gisborne, Thomas. *An Inquiry into the Duties of the Female Sex*. 7th ed. London: T. Cadell and W. Davies, 1801.

Graham, Walter. *English Literary Periodicals*. New York: T. Nelson & Sons, 1930.

———. *Tory Criticism in the Quarterly Review, 1809-1853*. New York: Columbia University Press, 1921.

Gregory, Allene. *The French Revolution and the English Novel*. New York: G. P. Putnam's Sons, 1915.

Gregory, Dr. John. *A Father's Legacy to His Daughters*. Boston: L. C. Bowles, 1822.

Halévy, Elie. *History of the English People*. 4 vols. New York: Harcourt, Brace and Co., 1924.

———. *A History of the English People in 1815*. London:

Penguin, 1924.

————. *A History of the English People in the Nineteenth Century*. 6 vols., 2d rev. ed. London: E. Benn, 1952.

Hamilton, Catherine J. *Women Writers: Their Works and Ways*. 1st ser. 1892. Reprint. New York: Books for Libraries Press, 1971.

Hamilton, Elizabeth. *The Cottagers of Glenburnie*. 3d ed. Edinburgh: Ballantyne, 1808.

————. *Letters on the Elementary Principles of Education*. 2 vols. London: Samuel Bishop, 1803.

————. *Memoirs of the Late Mrs. Elizabeth Hamilton with a Selection from her Correspondence and Other Unpublished Writings*. Edited by Elizabeth Ogilvy Benger. 2 vols. London: Longman, Hurst, Rees, Orme, Brown & Green, 1818.

Hamilton, Henry. *England: A History of the Homeland*. New York: W. W. Norton, 1948.

Hazlitt, William. *Lectures on the English Poets*. London: Taylor & Hessey, 1818.

Holbach, Paul Henri d'. *Système social*. Amsterdam: Londres, 1773.

Hopkins, Mary Alden. *Hannah More and Her Circle*. New York: Longmans, Green & Co., 1947.

Houghton, Walter E. *Victorian Frame of Mind*. New Haven, Conn.: Yale University Press, 1957.

Inchbald, Elizabeth. *A Simple Story*. 1796. Reprint. London: Oxford University Press, 1967.

Janeway, Elizabeth. *Man's World, Woman's Place: A Study in Social Mythology*. New York: Dell, 1971.

Jeffrey, Kirk. "The Family as Utopian Retreat from the City: The Nineteenth-Century Contribution." *The Family, Communes, and Utopian Societies*. Edited by Sallie TeSalle. New York: Harper & Row, 1971.

Johnson, Reginald Brimley. *The Women Novelists*. London: W. Collins Sons & Co., 1918.

Jones, Mary Gwladys. *Hannah More*. Cambridge: At the University Press, 1952.

Kiely, Robert. *The Romantic Novel in England*. Cambridge, Mass.: Harvard University Press, 1972.

Ladies Companion. London, 1837-40.

Ladies Garland. London, 1838.

Langdon-Davies, John. *A Short History of Women*. New York: Viking Press, 1927.

Laslett, Peter. *The World We Have Lost: England Before the Industrial Age*. 2d ed. New York: Scribners, 1973.

Locke, John. *The Educational Writings of John Locke*. Edited by James L. Axtell. Cambridge: At the University Press, 1968.

McGregor, O. R. "The Social Position of Women in England, 1850-1914." *British Journal of Sociology* 6 (March 1955): 48-60.

Marcus, Steven. *The Other Victorians: A Study of Sexuality and Pornography in Mid-Nineteenth-Century England*. New York: Basic Books, 1966.

Martineau, Harriet. *The History of England during the Thirty Years' Peace*. 2 vols. London: G. Bell & Sons, 1850.

Masefield, Muriel. *Women Novelists from Fanny Burney to George Eliot*. London: I. Nicholson & Watson, 1934.

Meliora: A Quarterly Review of Social Science, 1859-69. 12 vols. London, 1868.

Mitford, Mary Russell. *Our Village. The Works of Mary Russell Mitford, Prose and Verse*. Edited by Anne Thackeray Ritchie. London: Macmillan & Co., 1906.

Montesquieu, Baron Charles Louis de. *The Spirit of the Laws*. Translated by Thomas Nugent. New York: Appleton-Century-Crofts, 1949.

Monthly Mirror. London, 1799-1823.

Monthly Review, or Literary Journal. London, 1799-1815.

More, Hannah. *Coelebs in Search of a Wife*. 1809. Reprinted in *Collected Works*. 2 vols. New York: Harper & Bros., 1839.

―――. *The Complete Works of Hannah More*. 19 vols. New York: Harper & Bros., 1837.

―――. *Memoirs of the Life and Correspondence of Mrs. Hannah More*. Edited by William Roberts. 2 vols. New York: Harper & Bros., 1837.

―――. *Moral Sketches of Prevailing Opinions and Manners, Foreign and Domestic: With Reflections on Prayer. The Works of Hannah More.* 11 vols. London: T. Cadell, 1830. Vol. 4.

————. *Strictures on the Modern System of Female Education with a View to the Principles and Conduct of Women of Rank and Fortune. The Works of Hannah More.* 11 vols. London: T. Cadell, 1830. Vol. 5.

Morgan, Sydney Owenson. *The Wild Irish Girl.* 1806. Reprint. London: Chapman & Hall, 1936.

New Cambridge Bibliography of English Literature. Edited by George Watson. 4 vols. Cambridge: At the University Press, 1969.

Oliphant, Margaret. *The Literary History of England.* 3 vols. London: Macmillan & Co., 1894.

O'Neill, William L. *Divorce in the Progressive Era.* New Haven, Conn.: Yale University Press, 1967.

Opie, Amelia. *Father and Daughter. The Works of Mrs. Amelia Opie Complete in Three Volumes.* 8th ed. 1819. Reprint. Philadelphia: Crissy & Markley, 1850.

————. *Adeline Mowbray; or, The Mother and Daughter. The Works of Mrs. Amelia Opie Complete in Three Volumes.* 8th ed. 1819. Reprint. Philadelphia: Crissy & Markley, 1850.

Parsons, Eliza. *Mysterious Warnings.* 1796. Reprint. London: Folio Press, 1968.

Pennington, Sarah. *A Mother's Advice to Her Absent Daughters.* 1761. Reprint. Boston: L. C. Bowles, 1822.

Pinchbeck, Ivy. *Women Workers and the Industrial Revolution, 1750-1850.* London: Routledge, 1930.

Porter, Jane. *The Scottish Chiefs.* 1810. Reprint. Brattleborough: J. Holbrook, 1818.

Quarterly Review. London, 1809-24.

Quinlan, Maurice J. *The Victorian Prelude: A History of English Manners, 1700-1830.* New York: Columbia University Press, 1941.

Radcliffe, Ann. *The Mysteries of Udolpho.* London: G. G. & J. Robinson, 1794.

Reeve, Clara. *The Progress of Romance.* 1785. Reprint. New York: Facsimile Text Society, 1930.

Roberts, Helene E. "Marriage, Redundancy, or Sin."

Suffer and Be Still: Women in the Victorian Age. Edited by Martha E. Vicinus. Bloomington: University of Indiana Press, 1972.

Robertson, Priscilla. "Home as a Nest: Middle-Class Childhood in Nineteenth-Century Europe." *The History of Childhood.* Edited by Lloyd deMause. New York: Harper, 1974.

Rossi, Alice S. Introduction to *Mill's Essays on Sex Equality.* by John Stuart Mill and Harriet Taylor. Chicago: University of Chicago Press, 1970.

Rousseau, Jean Jacques. *Émile; or, Education.* Translated by Barbara Foxley. 1762. Reprint. New York: E. P. Dutton & Co., 1911.

————. *Rousseau on Education.* Edited by R. L. Archer. New York: Longmans, 1912.

Rowbotham, Sheila. *Hidden from History: Rediscovering Women in History from the Seventeenth Century to the Present.* New York: Pantheon, 1974.

Sandford, Mrs. John [Elizabeth Poole]. *Woman in Her Social and Domestic Character.* 2d ed. London: Longman, Rees, Orme, Brown, Green, and Longman, 1832.

Schneir, Miriam, ed. *Feminism: The Essential Historical Writings.* New York: Vintage, 1972.

Shelley, Mary. *Frankenstein.* 1818. Reprint. New York: Dell, 1965.

Sherwood, Mary Martha Butt. *The Life of Mrs. [Mary Martha Butt] Sherwood (chiefly autobiographical) with Extracts from Mr. Sherwood's Journal during His Imprisonment in France and Residence in India.* Edited by her daughter, Sophia Kelly. London: Darton, 1854.

————. *The Life of Mrs. Sherwood Written by Herself with Extracts from Mr. Sherwood's Journal during his Imprisonment in France and Residence in India.* Abridged from London edition. Boston: American Tract Society, 1864.

————. *Susan Gray.* 1802. Reprint. Wellington: F. Houlston & Son, 1828.

Shine, Hill, and Shine, Helen Chadwick. *The Quarterly Review under Gifford.* Chapel Hill: University of North Carolina Press, 1949.

Stanhope, Lady Hester. *Life and Letters of Lady Hester Stanhope by Her Niece, the Duchess of Cleveland.* London: Clowes, 1897.

————. *Memoirs of the Lady Hester Stanhope as Related by Herself in Conversations with Her Physician, Charles Lewis Meryon.* 3 vols. London: H. Colburn, 1845.

Stenton, Doris. *The English Woman in History.* New York: Macmillan Co., 1957.

Stevenson, Lionel. *The English Novel: A Panorama.* Boston: Houghton Mifflin Co., 1960.

————. *The Wild Irish Girl: The Life of Sydney Owenson, Lady Morgan, 1776-1859.* London: Chapman & Hall, 1936.

Strachey, Ray. *"The Cause": A Short History of the Women's Movement in Great Britain.* London: G. Bell & Sons, 1928.

Taylor, Ann. *Practical Hints to Young Females on The Duties of a Wife, a Mother, and a Mistress of a Family.* 3d ed. London: Taylor & Hessey, 1815.

Taylor, Isaac. *Memoirs and Political Remains of the Late Jane Taylor with Extracts from Her Correspondence.* Philadelphia, Pa.: J. J. Woodward, 1827.

Thompson, Edward P. *The Making of the English Working Class.* New York: Vintage, 1963.

Thompson, William. *An Appeal of One Half of the Human Race, Women, against the Pretensions of the Other Half, Men, to Retain Them in Political and Thence in Civil and Domestic Slavery; in Reply to a Paragraph of Mr. Mill's Celebrated "Article on Government."* London: Longman, Hurst, Rees, Orme, Brown & Green, 1825.

Tompkins, Joyce Marjorie Sanxter. *The Popular Novel in England, 1770-1800.* London: Constable & Co., 1932.

Trimmer, Sarah. *Easy Lessons; or, Leading Strings to Knowledge in Three Parts: The First and Third Parts by a Lady for Her Own Children: The Second Part Arranged by the Late Mrs. Trimmer.* London: Harris, 1838.

Walker, Alexander. *Woman Physiologically Considered as to Mind, Morals, Marriage, Matrimonial Slavery, Infidelity, and Divorce.* 1839. Reprint. Hartford, Conn.: Andrus, 1854.

Wallace, William Ross. *The Battle of Tippicanoe and Triumphs of Science and Other Poems.* Cincinnati, Ohio: McFarlin, 1837.

Wasserstrom, William. *Heiress of All the Ages: Sex and Sentiment in the Genteel Tradition.* Minneapolis: University of Minnesota Press, 1959.

Webb, Robert. *Modern England: From the Eighteenth Century to the Present.* New York: Dodd, Mead & Co., 1971.

Weber, Eugen. *A Modern History of Europe.* New York: W. W. Norton, 1971.

Welter, Barbara. "The Cult of True Womanhood: 1820-1860." *American Quarterly* 18 (1966).

West, Jane. *The Advantages of Education; or, The History of Maria Williams.* London: Minerva Press, 1803.

―――. *Letters to a Young Lady in Which the Duties and Character of Women Are Considered, Chiefly with a Reference to Prevailing Opinions.* 4th ed. 3 vols. London: Longman, Hurst, Rees, Orme & Brown, 1806.

Willy, Margaret. *Three Women Diarists.* London: Longmans, 1964.

Wilson, Mona. *These Were Muses.* London: Sidgwick, 1924.

Wollstonecraft, Mary. *A Vindication of the Rights of Women.* 1792. Reprint. New York: E. P. Dutton & Co., 1929.

―――. *On the Vindication of the Rights of Women.* 2 vols. 1792. Reprint. London: Walter Scott, 1891.

―――. *Thoughts on the Education of Daughters with Reflections on Female Conduct, in the More Important Duties of Life.* London: J. Johnson, 1787.

Woolf, Virginia. *A Room of One's Own.* 1929. Reprint. New York: Harcourt, Brace & Co., 1957.

―――. *The Common Reader.* 2d ser. London: Hogarth Press, 1932.

Wordsworth, Dorothy. *Journals of Dorothy Wordsworth.* Edited by Ernest de Selincourt. 2 vols. London: Macmillan & Co., 1941.

Wordsworth, William. *The Complete Poetical Works of William Wordsworth.* Edited by Andrew J. George. Cambridge: At the University Press, 1932.

Index